The Quite Possible She

The Quite Possible She

Today's Christian Woman

Janet Golden

HERDER AND HERDER

1966
HERDER AND HERDER NEW YORK
232 Madison Avenue, New York 10016

Library of Congress Catalog Card Number: 66–22602
© 1966 by Herder and Herder, Inc.
Manufactured in the United States of America

Yes, I rise to defend
The quite possible She.
For the feminine gend-
Er is O.K. by me.
PHYLLIS MCGINLEY

Contents

The Quite Possible She

Any author entering a field as densely and formidably occupied as that of books about woman is tempted to offer a word of explanation. The question that irresistibly springs to mind when one hears of such a project, even if one is too polite to express it, is: Why another? Perhaps I should leave other authors to defend themselves, but it seems to me that there are at least three more or less sound reasons for adding to an already substantial deposit.

In the first place, books about contemporary women tend to become outdated with discouraging rapidness. A decade would be an unusually long life span, and five years or less is closer to the mark. The second reason is that, with a subject so vast as half the human race, there are always new aspects and approaches to explore and take, and special audiences to be addressed.

Perhaps more persuasive than either of these reasons, however, is the simple desire to have the last word on a subject that lends itself to polemics. Even writers securely established in other fields may sooner or later find themselves defending or attacking some aspect of femininity. A recent example of such a person is Phyllis McGinley, who has been described by *Time* as "almost by inadvertence . . . the sturdiest exponent of the glory of housewifery, standing almost alone against a rising chorus of voices summoning women away from the hearth."[1]

When I began writing this book in the early spring of 1963, I had an uneasy feeling that *The Feminine Mystique*, which had triggered it, was likely to set off an avalanche of books and magazine articles on the married woman's role which would make the normal increase in writing on the subject seem trivial. Nevertheless, the problem which Mrs. Friedan has raised of the "empty years" in a married woman's life, the years after her children have left home, seemed to me to be something which merited but had never received discussion from a Christian point of view. Still more significant, there was really no over-all view in Catholic writing of the working out of a vocation to marriage over a *whole* lifetime. It seemed to me, therefore, that in order to discuss the gap in the pattern, the "empty years," I would be obliged to attempt a book of this kind, which saw the pattern, or patterns, as a whole. The life-begins-at-forty book might have an immediate appeal to a rather neglected Catholic audience, but at the cost of ignoring the fact that what a woman is at forty, depends markedly on what she was and did at twenty and thirty.

Such a book could not be dashed off, particularly as I had no intention of producing a personal manifesto. In a certain sense the book would be a personal one—I was close to forty, married, and a mother; but I was not tempted to autobiography, and I mistrust the easy slide from private experience to "We women . . ."

[1] Cover story, "The Telltale Hearth," June 18, 1965.

Moreover, it seemed in fact most improbable that I could arrive at a generally useful notion of over-all patterns in married women's lives, the balance of various interests and elements, simply by taking myself as an example, and straining out the more obvious singularities of my situation. This sort of pruning can produce a very unreal and lopsided image of housewifery. A decent amount of introspection was necessary, but I felt that it should be balanced by testing and enlarging my own experience and observations against a wide range of findings from various fields and against opinions that differed markedly from my own.

Inevitably, all this did take time, and I am particularly grateful for the patience of my publishers, who saw the first draft late in 1963, and encouraged me to work it out carefully, without the pressure of deadlines, over almost two more years. I am equally grateful for the patience, not to say tolerance, of my family during a seemingly interminable work-in-progress. The writing may have been kept to "off-duty" hours, but the absentmindedness brought on by thinking and rethinking each step could not, and in time they learned to say everything to me twice.

Acknowledgements and appreciations could easily take a chapter in themselves, for a book like this one is begun long before its formal starting date, and threatens to go on indefinitely. I shall condense them, then, by thanking the true instigators of this book, my parents, sister, friends, and many of my teachers—all those who encouraged me to believe that "growing up female" could be not only worthwhile, but also a not too self-conscious process.

Lafayette, California   JANET GOLDEN

I

The Changing World of the Housewife

This is not a book about Woman. Altogether too much has already been written and said about Woman, and here one must also include what has been said about such sub-species as Christian Woman, Modern Woman, even that less impressive figure, the American Housewife.

In the first place, if one hopes to speak to women, and not merely about them, it is better to avoid such lofty collectives. The woman who still has the faint hope of reading something which might be applicable to her own case, finds wholesale prescriptions and splendid generalities about "woman's nature" irritating or at least soporiferous. She does not now and no doubt never did want to hear that

> *Women are this or that.*
> *Woman is round, or high, or square, or flat.*[1]

Nevertheless, some generalizations, however exasperating they may be, are impossible to avoid. It is hoped that, in spite of their occasionally obtrusive presence, it will remain clear that this book is written for and about individuals, not about faceless Woman.

Moreover, our subject, however unmanageable it may

[1] Anna Wickham, "Friend Cato."

prove to be, is relatively modest and specific in comparison to books about Woman. If we were to pick an individual woman who would most closely approximate its focal point, she would be the educated Catholic married woman, perhaps the wife of an "emerging layman," but not necessarily of the new generation born after 1930. She might just as appropriately have been born in the Twenties, and be turning over in her mind what it means to be that little-studied figure, the middle-aged American housewife. Indeed, it may be that it is to the woman approaching middle age that this book speaks most directly, for the very young may find a rather long-term view of life presently somewhat unreal and removed from their current preoccupations; and on the other hand, older women may see our emphasis on choice an irrelevant one precluded by circumstance.

But whatever her age, our "subject" is at least half aware that there is little agreement both about what she is and what she should be. Is she, for instance, what Betty Friedan regards her to be, a singularly handicapped example of the "trapped" housewife? Mrs. Friedan writes with assurance that "Women of orthodox Catholic or Jewish origin do not easily break through the housewife image; it is enshrined in the canons of their religion, in the assumptions of their own and their husbands' childhoods, and in their church's [sic] dogmatic definitions of marriage and motherhood."[2]

Or is this "housewife image" not so unchanging after all, and do not many American housewives belong to the "new type," the modern woman who has been thus described by Cardinal Léon-Joseph Suenens: "She does not

[2] *The Feminine Mystique*, W. W. Norton, New York, 1963, p. 351.

passively accept her fate, she takes charge of it. Freed from her former shackles, she develops in an atmosphere that allows her to make use of her natural gifts. Greater life expectation gives her, once her children are grown up, an extra life as it were. The culture available to her is wider and she has more leisure. All these new factors affect her position and activities in the world and open up an almost unlimited opportunity for expansion."[3]

Should this picture encourage her, the American Catholic housewife is then reminded by at least one spokeswoman, Solange Hertz, that "expansion" and "emergence" are quite counter to her vocation. Mrs. Hertz writes, "The married woman . . . is a cloistered woman . . . the wife and mother's life is fundamentally an enclosed one of prayer, service, and suffering."[4] Altogether, therefore, the role of the educated Catholic married woman is not a clear one in the minds of educated Catholic married women. She is more often exhorted to understand herself than she is understood. Nor is it always plain to her or to her exhorters that the problems and opportunities which she faces are new.

If she is faced with change, however, and with perplexity about her role, that in no way makes her peculiarly unfortunate, or even distinctive. She is part of a changing society, a changing world, a changing Church. Her unique predicament is only a part of the "ordeal of change" that has characterized this and the last century. In fact, perhaps the only thing which really distinguishes the "woman problem"

[3] *The Nun in the World*, Newman, Westminster, 1963, p. 11.
[4] *Searcher of Majesty*, Newman, Westminster, 1963, pp. 214–215.

from any other is the persistent notion that there must be some one solution to it which will fit all women, if not for all time, at least for the time being.

Important as it is to keep in mind that women have not been particularly victimized in the course of history, it is still necessary for us to go into some detail about the way recent history has affected women's life and work. Apart from this background, any discussion about the changes taking place in the role of married women today is lacking in convincingness and perspective.

Even deciding where to begin in sketching the simplest background is a problem. We are, as Karl Rahner says, in the midst of a "breaking up of things" involving, as it does in many important respects, "lumping together all past periods as one by contrast with that which is approaching."[5] For women, this "breaking up," which coincided more or less with the Industrial Revolution, precipitated far-reaching changes in the whole pattern, the very equilibrium of their lives.[6] But it was by no means a uniform change which took place, and women in a number of countries— America was one of them—adhered to much of the pre-industrial way of life until close to the end of the nine-teenth century.

Whether it came quickly or slowly, this change was not, as some feminists have attempted to picture it, simply a transition from slavery and subjection to a new equality

[5] *The Christian Commitment*, Sheed and Ward, New York, 1963, p. 133.

[6] Mirra Komarovsky has observed that "Women became a 'social problem' because technological and social changes over the past century and a half have disturbed the old equilibrium without as yet replacing it with another." *Women in the Modern World*, Little, Brown, Boston, 1953, p. 48.

and emancipation. In the breaking-up brought about by industrialism, much was being lost by women that their gain of franchise, legal rights, and entrance into male professions could not restore to them.

Any attempt to survey women's activities and statuses down through the centuries would be a book in itself, and a quite redundant one at that.[7] What is worth-while dwelling on for a moment, however, if we are to understand the situation of married women in America today, are those incredibly rapid changes which have taken place quite recently—within the lifetime of our parents.

We are obliged, of course, in such a sketching in, to deal with the typical and the average. To take the most obvious point, woman's life-span is now much longer. The generation of young women now entering college has a twenty-one-year greater life expectancy than the generation born in 1900.[8] The most significant aspect of this change is that it has not meant more years of old age and debility, but rather an extension of the years of middle life.

In almost every respect, the distribution of her years has changed for the average American woman. In 1890, she left school at the age of 14, and there was a long stretch of about eight years during which she went to work or helped at home before marriage in her early twenties.[9] By the

[7] We recommend, however, Mary Beard's Woman as Force in History, Macmillan, 1946.

[8] American Women, A Report of the President's Commission on the Status of Women, Washington, D.C., 1963, p. 58.

[9] In 1890, "about half of all women worked for pay outside the home during part of the eight to ten years after they left school and before they were married." Robert M. Smuts, Women and Work in America, Columbia University Press, New York, 1959, p. 23.

1950's, the median age for these events had changed so radically that there was only a scant two years between the end of school at 18, and marriage, then at 20, rather than at 22. Just as the period of work before marriage is now likely to be much shorter, so too is the period devoted to child-bearing and child-rearing shorter by an average of five years. If the earlier marriage age is taken into account, this means that the married woman of today sees her youngest child entering school when she is only 32, while her counterpart of 1900 reached this turning point at 39.

Common sense indicates that we are on safer ground in generalizing about the length of years spent in education than on the period spent in bearing and raising a family. A longer period of education is typical for most women today, while variations in the years devoted to child-bearing are wide. Particularly in discussions concerning Catholic women, it would be somewhat unrealistic were we to assume that child-bearing (with a safe statistical average of about three children) is over at the age of 26. But the tendency towards a longer period of education, earlier marriage, a smaller family, and a freer, longer period of middle age runs through society, and it affects the Catholic married woman, if in no other way, as a norm which she may feel herself to be out of step with.

Still another change in the life pattern, and one which is gaining in momentum, is the tendency for the middle-aged married woman to enter the working world. Simply the presence of a substantial number of married women in the work force is a marked contrast to the pattern at the turn of the century, when even among the poorest slum workers, only a family catastrophe, a husband's illness, incapacity, or desertion would force a wife and mother to go out to work. The change in pattern has been a gradual one, encouraged by the demand for women workers during two world wars and the improvement in working conditions and job opportunities. But perhaps the most striking aspect of the change has been in the age of the women who work. As the President's Commission on the Status of Women reported, the change in the proportion of married women in the female work force from less than a third in 1940 to more than half in 1962 was largely due to the number of women over 45 who chose to go to work.[10]

Charts and statistics on median ages, however, give only a spare picture of the change in married women's lives, and sometimes a misleading one. While it is perfectly true, for instance, that the average family today is smaller than it was in 1890, these figures are somewhat meaningless for a woman who either makes no attempt to space her children, or is unable to do so. Because of the decline in infant mortality and deaths among young children, she would be likely to have more rather than less children than her grandmother.

We are on much solider ground with regard to the changes that have taken place in the work that goes on in the home, for here we can point to an apparently straight line of progress in the lightening and simplifying of manual work. In 1890, the only commonly used mechanical helps

[10] Between 1920 and 1960 the percentage of working women from 25 to 44 has stayed about the same, but the groups under 25 and those 45 and over has been completely reversed. In 1920 about 40 per cent of all women workers were under 25 and less than 20 per cent were women over 45. By 1960, these figures had changed places. *American Women*, p. 66.

in housekeeping were the egg beater and the sewing machine, while many middle-class housewives today take
automatic washing machines and driers for granted, and
may have progressed to the ultimate refinement of electric
can-openers and egg cookers. A still more fundamental
easing of the burden of housework has come with central
heating, and hot and cold running water. In 1890, women
were stoking and cleaning the stoves that heated the house.
If they wanted hot water, it would first have to be brought
in from an outside well or a tap down the hall, and then
heated on the kitchen fire.

The range of activities that once made up what is so
euphemistically called homemaking seems almost fantastic
by today's standards, and, of course, the contrast is greater
when one examines the farm woman of the last century.
Even if there was no question of field work, this woman
probably raised the family's fruit and vegetable foods in a
kitchen garden and preserved them for winter use. Butter-
churning, molasses-making, care of poultry were among
her other tasks. She might also have made such things as
brooms, mattresses, and soap; she certainly made most of
the clothes for her family, and mended and laundered
them.

The farm wife was the prototypical housewife of the last
century. Even in 1890, with the move to the cities well
under way, half of all American women were still living on
farms.

But the days of the city woman, who is more likely to be
the grandmother of today's Catholic housewife, were busy,
too. A surprising number raised some of the food for their
families; and the care of urban poultry pens and gardens

when men worked outside the home, ten and twelve hours a day, was woman's work.[11] In any case, however, garden or not, much of the time-consuming food processing of the rural woman was the urban woman's task as well, and she also had such chores to carry out as stove-tending, cleaning, and sewing; and like the farm wife, she was responsible for most of the medical care of her family. In addition, a good many city women took on extra work at home for pay, most often by letting rooms to boarders or as seamstresses.

The path leading from the humble egg-beater to the electric stove that turns itself on, cooks dinner, turns off, and even cleans itself, is not, however, a straight line of progress. It gives this impression only by leaving out some negative factors, but these are also part of the picture of change. One is the question of who tends the stove, be it wood-burner or electric wonder. If the question were asked in 1890, there might have been a number of answers given: an older daughter, a maiden aunt or grandmother, a hired girl, or the housewife herself. Were the question asked to-day, the answer, with no options, would be the housewife. Full-time help no longer costs five dollars a week; older daughters are in high school or college; and the "extended family" populated by grandparents and maiden aunts belongs to the past. The housewife's work is lightened from a mechanical point of view, but the work is all hers and she now works alone. If she comes from a middle- or upper-class background, the contrast may seem very sharp to her between her once-a-week cleaning woman, and the full-

---

[11] "Except in the crowded tenement districts of the large cities —which housed a small fraction of the total urban population— town and city dwellers often produced some of their own food." Robert M. Smuts, *Women and Work in America*, p. 11.

time help she remembers from the home of her mother.

Loneliness is one troublesome factor that has come with change. More intangible is a growing sense of triviality, and triviality mixes poorly with housewifery—or anything else —unless it comes in as a grace note to a more serious theme. Homemaking may be made up of small and oddly assorted tasks, but the comfort in them for the woman involved has been the idea that they—and she herself—are necessary. When making dinner involves opening cans and heating frozen foods in a matter of minutes, a sense of triviality necessarily enters in. It becomes irritating as well when the housewife realizes that the dinner carefully prepared in two and a half hours could have been made in half an hour with packaged foods costing only twenty-five cents more.[12]

There is something unsettling in realizing that at least part of one's daily labors works out to a financial equivalent of five cents an hour, or, alternatively, could be performed by any child tall enough to reach the stove. Indeed, it was the burden of triviality, beginning to weigh heavily on middle-class English and American women in Victorian times, that may have been chiefly responsible for the wave of change brought about by feminism. In that period, the appearance of affluence demanded the presence of demonstrably idle womenfolk about the home, who could neither

[12] A study by the Department of Food and Nutrition of the Drexel Institute of Technology prepared seven menus in two ways: with home-prepared ingredients and packaged foods in quantities that would serve four. "The average meal made from convenience foods costs only 23 cents more than the same meal made from home-prepared ingredients and takes one fourth the time to prepare." "Spend & Save," in Ladies' Home Journal, June, 1964.

go out to work, nor set their hands to any kind of domestic task. Feminism in some form would probably have arisen to correct the obvious political, economic, and legal injustices in the treatment of women during the last century; but the crusading fervor and the animosity towards men which characterized the feminist crusades, was in good part a reaction to imposed idleness, to an oppressive sense of triviality.

The specific goals which feminism attained are part of the changed world of the Christian married woman today. She may vote, run for political office, earn an advanced degree in a university, and enter almost any profession. And yet in practice, with the possible exception of the franchise, the typical American woman may have very little more effect on the world around her than did her grandmother. To the anguish of neo-feminists, and the perplexity of more detached observers, the post-war generation of American women, who had the intellectual and financial capacity to take advantage of new opportunities, chose early marriage and motherhood—and this choice was deliberate.

The most obvious example of this shift in values was the decline of the proportion of women among college students. In 1920, they represented 47 per cent of all students; in 1958, only 35 per cent. Still more noticeable was the falling off in those taking higher degrees. Women took one in seven of the doctoral degrees in 1920, but by 1956, one in ten.[13]

Even so, no evaluation of change in women's lives can stop with the tangible results, or lack of results, of the

[13] John Henry Cutler, *What about Women?*, Ives Washburn, New York, 1961, p. 89.

feminist program. As a movement, it was concerned not only with specific rights, but with the underlying fact that women were truly *persons*, who were entitled to expect as one consequence, the ordinary political and social rights accorded to human persons in their society. It is this aspect of feminism, with its accompanying liability of somewhat hazy distinctions between the masculine and the feminine, which has had some of the subtlest and most far-reaching effects on women's lives today.

Individual consciousness, the sense of oneself as a person, is not easily measured in graphs and statistics. It cannot properly be confined to the limit of a movement such as feminism, nor, for that matter, be attributed to only one sex. One notable aspect of human development in Western society in the past few centuries has been men's increased sense of themselves as autonomous and unique beings. It is within this context that feminism and the wider development of individual consciousness in women must be placed. Ignace Lepp has formulated the problem thus: "Not so long ago women were very proud of their mission to be the servant of the species. Today they are conscious of themselves as *persons*, and desire for themselves all that goes along with being a person, namely, independence, freedom, the right to happiness, and the right to individual development. Men have been animated for a long time by the same desires, but from now on they will not be able to satisfy these desires except in relation to those of their feminine companions.[14]

Quite obviously, this aspect of change is not limited to such matters as the number of women who actually take

[14] *The Psychology of Loving*, Helicon, Baltimore, 1963, p. 138.

advanced degrees and enter professions. It is a changing attitude which underlies the recent emphasis on domesticity as well as on the entrance of women into the working world. Difficult though it may be to measure and analyze, it is an ever present factor in women's lives today, and one that defies any merely mechanical redistribution of women's time and energy. If women are searching for a new equilibrium, a new patterning of their lives, such a pattern, or patterns, will have to take into account not just the change in the milieu of married life, but the change in the woman herself who experiences it. She is not just her grandmother in a short skirt and a mechanized kitchen.

Solutions both highly specific and enormously general are being proposed for the problems which change has brought into the life of the American married woman today. She is being asked, or told, to stay home with her children and bake her own bread, or urged to start looking for housekeepers and day-care centers for her offspring so that she can find what Betty Friedan calls the "fourth dimension," that is, woman's own identity in society.[15]

In the fairly recent past, the solutions proposed seemed to oscillate between adopting one or the other of two extreme models, the "career woman," heroine of the feminists who regarded motherhood and domesticity as a trap; and the traditional housewife and mother, who limited her interests to raising her own family. In at least a limited sense, the career woman seemed to have caught the imagination of middle-class America in the pre-World War II years. But if the college drop-outs, the decline of interest in

[15] Betty Friedan, "Woman: The Fourth Dimension," in *Ladies' Home Journal*, June, 1964. This article somewhat modifies the position taken in *The Feminine Mystique*.

advanced training, the lower age for marriage, and the larger families of the post-war period are indications, the image of the traditional housewife has been in the ascendancy in more recent years.

However, neither image offers wholly satisfactory solutions because, for the most part, women who have a choice will put raising a family first in their lives, first in importance, and first in time. Needless to say, this cuts the ground out from under any masculine-patterned career plan: men, in a competitive world, do not drop out of college and take a ten to twenty-year leave of absence from their chosen field. As for the totally domesticated woman, many housewives, whether they are baking their own bread with stone-ground flour or heating TV dinners, have an uncomfortable feeling that a nineteenth-century pattern of living is not solving their problems.

At the present time, various attempts are being made to bridge the gap between the feminist and the traditional ideals for women. Among neo-feminists, there is the admission, however grudging, that even intelligent and educated women want families of their own, and are willing to sacrifice professional advantages in order to raise them. Among neo-traditionalists, there is the growing awareness that raising a family may not absorb the whole range of a woman's attention, and the entire span of her years. In practice, this has meant such relatively new phenomena as opportunities for "continuing education" at a college level and for advanced degrees for women in their forties and fifties; an increased emphasis on part-time work for women; and a steadily mounting proportion of middle-aged women in the working world.

But neither in theory nor in practice is there any real

unanimity as to where this "middle ground" should be situated. The underlying assumptions in the two camps are still too different for any thoroughgoing consensus. Many neo-feminists still seem to regard motherhood as a sort of biological obstacle course on the way to true fulfill-ment in a career. A neo-traditionalist may regard work out-side the home, whether paid or volunteer, as a sort of last resort for the middle-aged woman not sensible enough to be still occupied with her tenth or twelfth child, or a flock of grandchildren. Even on the very practical point of when children no longer need the undivided attention of their mother, there is no agreement: ". . . many psychiatrists, social workers, and church leaders maintain that the emotional development of children is endangered when mothers spend time at work rather than at home. . . . Sup-porters of this view generally agree, however, that children are no longer endangered by their mother's absence once they reach a certain age, which has been set as low as three and as high as eighteen."[16]

It is this changed world, with its criss-cross of opinion and practice, its tentative solutions, that the Catholic married woman inhabits today. More than in any other time in history, she is exposed to every jolt of public opinion and public practice. The Church to which she be-longs is, to use the description of Karl Rahner, the "Church of the diaspora." Quite simply, this means that she cannot expect her faith to be supported and borne effortlessly along by custom and law, governmental decree, or a clearly defined public opinion. To a degree unprecedented in the past, she must "achieve" her faith rather than accept it.

[16] Robert W. Smuts, Women and Work in America, p. 152.

If this is true of Christian faith in general, it is equally true of a Christian concept of marriage, the lay vocation, and the nature of woman. Nor are these academic matters. On her view of them, grounded in faith, hang innumerable practical decisions and eternal consequences. Somehow, and rather quickly, she must separate what is of permanent value in the traditional Christian view and what can be safely jettisoned as social means used to implement that value in a given period. Without such discrimination, change may be bolted down heedlessly, regardless of its effect on fundamental values, or disastrously resisted when the need for new social means is imperative.

To separate the permanent from the passing, to win through to a Christian view appropriate for her own time of women, of their role in marriage, and of their vocation as lay persons, is not easy. If she turns to the literature on the subject for help she will find a small library of books on marriage, woman, the laity, child-raising, the meaning of sex in marriage, and only a small handful, mostly European, which discuss some of the problems of change in women's lives. Even the books in this last category, however, do not approach the subject from the angle which may be most crucial for the individual woman, that is, from an integrated point of view which attempts to take in the entire span of her life, including middle and old age and the entire range of her activities over the course of these years.

Books about the young wife and mother, as well as scattered materials which have a bearing on the later stages of her life and further aspects of her activity, are to be found everywhere, but there has been no attempt made at synthesis. The more one investigates the material on a Christian view of the married woman, the clearer it becomes that a view which is both comprehensive and personal is impossible to find. Indeed, it does not exist. The raw materials, the various elements are there, but so widely scattered that the majority of women, preoccupied with their problems on a practical level, will feel obliged to let someone else's theory and their own practice remain at a distance.

It is not likely that a synthesis will be made very soon or be the work of a single person. Various exploratory attempts, including a few by those amateurs among experts, the Christian married women themselves,[17] will be needed before a clear picture and a program—or programs—can truly come into being. This book represents such a partial venture. If this is indeed the age of the laity, then it is time to explore more fully what this fact should mean to an educated Catholic wife and mother—what, in this country, at this time, are her dilemmas and opportunities.

[17] A series begun in *Ave Maria* in September, 1964, "The New Catholic Woman," was such a venture.

II

The Quite Possible She

Any discussion which involves women, no matter how limited its scope, be it about women's hats, their politics, or their education, is likely to end as an impassioned controversy on woman's nature. A cautious author would be well advised to circle around a subject on which so much information and so little agreement exist, but no matter how circumspectly the problem is approached, it cannot be evaded. Theorizing about the role of married women today, in or out of the home, necessarily also involves theorizing about women themselves.

To take as starting point for this consideration Phyllis McGinley's "quite possible She"—

> Yes, I rise to defend
> The quite possible She.
> For the feminine gend-
> Er is O.K. by me[1]—

is not so frivolous as it at first glance might seem. Whatever one's notions may be about women, it is clear that

[1] *Times Three*, The Viking Press, New York, 1961; from "Why Some of My Best Friends Are Women," p. 226.

their possibilities are more various than most theorists of the past would have suspected. A woman today may be a cosmonaut or a Nobel Prize-winner in physics, and she may attempt to combine either of these unusual careers with the traditional role of wife and mother. She may even become an anthropologist and further complicate the picture by showing the vastly different ways in which it is possible for cultures to interpret the differences between the two sexes. Anthropologist Margaret Mead has thus given her view of the problem: "Some peoples think of women as too weak to work out of doors, others regard women as the appropriate bearers of heavy burdens, 'because their heads are stronger than man's.' . . . Whether we deal with small matters or with large, with the frivolities of ornament and cosmetics or the sanctities of man's place in the universe, we find this great variety of ways, often flatly contradictory one to the other, in which the roles of the two sexes have been patterned."[2]

The range of the "possible She" is an embarrassment to some theorists and a delight to others, but in any case it is there, and has to be taken into account.

For a Christian woman who wants to find her bearings in this complicated subject, a natural beginning is to look at Scripture. Genesis will tell her nothing at all about X and Y chromosomes or the Terman-Miles Masculinity-Femininity Index, but it can tell her of the basic relationship of men and women to each other and to God:

So God created man in his own image, in the image of God he created him; male and female he created them. . . .

[2] Male and Female. A Study of the Sexes in a Changing World, William Morrow, New York, 1949; Mentor Books edition, p. 16.

Then the Lord God said, "It is not good that the man should be alone; I will make a helper fit for him."

So out of the ground the Lord God formed every beast of the field and every bird of the air . . . but for the man there was not found a helper fit for him.

So the Lord God caused a deep sleep to fall upon the man, and while he slept took one of his ribs and closed up its place with flesh; and the rib which the Lord God had taken from the man he made into a woman and brought her to the man.

Then the man said,

> "This at last is bone of my bones
>   and flesh of my flesh;
> and she shall be called Woman,
>   because she was taken out of man."

Therefore a man leaves his father and his mother and cleaves to his wife, and they become one flesh.

[Gen. 1, 27; 2, 18, 20, 21–24]

What is it that these few verses from the two creation accounts in *Genesis* really tell us about woman's nature? There is the temptation of the theorist on women, scanning them for ammunition, to settle on one particular aspect, woman's dignity, for instance, or her subordination. It would be best, therefore, to concentrate on the larger truth contained here, which is quite simply that the woman, like her husband, is a human person, possessing the same nature; that both together constitute the human species man, who is "in the image of God." In the plan of God, she is to be a helper to man, his natural complement and partner, and in marriage, dependent on him. It is on this rather spare but nevertheless profoundly important foundation that a Christian view of the married woman must be built. It rules out from the start any notion of woman as a different and inferior sort of species, man's chattel and slave, his "first domestic animal." On the contrary, she is man's companion, sharing in the dignity of being created in God's image. Self-evident as this might seem from a religious point of view, it was actually a revolutionary idea if one takes into account the rather low estimate of women expressed in the major non-Christian religions, particularly of the Far East. Respect for woman as an individual is evidently not an essential aspect of religious experience as the various world religions have known it.

While modern American women are not in need of assurance that they are not chattels, the notion of woman as helper to man, and as dependent on him in marriage, is relevant to some of their problems. Such notions are the foundation of a consideration of the married laywoman, just as the vocation to a Christian life is the superstructure.

But one has to admit that the foundations, firm though they are, leave a rather wide range for building. The greater part of the building up of theory, if not of practice, in the past could best be passed over in regretful silence. *Genesis* did not pretend to teach biology, but mistaken notions of women's nature based on *Genesis* have hampered a realistic concept of woman down to our own day. This biological error has often resulted in seeing woman as "a man without procreative power, a 'misbegotten,' mutilated, degenerate male."[3]

Admittedly, this biological view of woman is more of a curiosity than a problem today. The great difficulty now in evaluating the nature of women derives from conflicts within the social sciences. Detailed information on women

[3] F. X. Arnold, *Woman and Man*, Herder and Herder, New York, 1963, p. 33.

could theoretically provide a basis for a middle-ground approach to understanding woman, and it is encouraging to find that where there is disagreement, at least about relative intelligence of the sexes, it is not particularly rancorous.[4]

Nevertheless, there is a very sharp difference between the way in which feminists, past and present, and those who support a more traditional view of women, select and evaluate the available facts. In the process of this selection the middle ground too often gets lost, and what emerges is an insistence either on the similarities between men and women, or on the differences. Although there have been marked differences of opinion within the respective groups, particularly within the feminist camp, one is more than likely to find feminists stressing the near identity of the two sexes, and traditionalists the contrasts.

These two viewpoints are not always spelled out, but there are some writers, generally clerics, who will take pains to clarify the matter: ". . . the feminists have generally held Plato's basic premise: I. Save in their primary sexual functions men and women are identical. Their two main conclusions, as Plato's, have therefore been: II. In work, education, and social mores the sexes should likewise be considered identical and any custom to the contrary should be credited to mere cultural slavish imposi-

[4] The following quotations are from two writers with markedly different views on the nature of woman: "As far as science knows, men and women's basic intellectual potentials are identical." Lucius F. Cervantes, S.J., *Marriage and the Family*, Regnery, Chicago, 1956, p. 508. ". . . conclusive proof as to innate differences in mental aptitudes of the sexes may not be forthcoming for years to come. . . . If ever confirmed, these inborn differences will be small." Komarovsky, *Women in the Modern World*, p. 29.

tion. III. Institutionalized and socially enforced monog-army, using such stereotypes as "woman the homemaker, man the breadwinner," is likewise a mere cultural imposition that can perfectly well be forgotten."[5] Interestingly, this priest-author feels that it is "the foundation of the institution of marriage itself which is at stake" when the differences are to be emphasized: ". . . the male is the more dominant sex in the physical sphere by virtue of his motor-muscular-aggressive credentials and . . . a woman is not a small man but essentially an individual whose glory is her maternal nature." "To understand the mother is to understand the woman."[6]

It should not be assumed that the author, Father Lucius Cervantes, is attacking some imaginary or long-deceased opponents. It is in fact no compliment to most women to tell them that, in understanding motherhood, they have understood womanhood as well. Most women resent the suggestion. One recent writer, Alice Rossi, pictures a woman of the future who is unquestionably not going to be explained in terms of motherhood: "Marriage for our hypothetical woman will not mark a withdrawal from the life and work pattern that she has established. . . . She will have few children if she does have them, and will view her pregnancies, childbirth, and early months of motherhood as one among many equally important highlights in her life."[7]

[5] Cervantes, Marriage and the Family, p. 160.
[6] Ibid., pp. 137, 333, 234.
[7] "Equality between the Sexes: An Immodest Proposal," in Daedalus, Spring, 1964. This well-documented study is useful as a clear and compact expression of modern feminism carried to its logical conclusion. A recent article in The American Scholar, "An

If "early months of motherhood" sounds odd, it is to be explained by an earlier suggestion: "If a reserve of trained practical mothers were available," Mrs. Rossi writes, "a professional woman could return to her field a few months after the birth of a child, leaving the infant under the care of a practical mother until he or she reached the age of two years, at about which age the child could enter a child-care center for daytime care. Assuming a two-child family, this could mean not more than one year of withdrawal from her professional field for the working mother."[8]

Obviously, there are very sharp differences of opinion about the fundamental nature of woman.

Perhaps the best way to evaluate these differences is to begin by discerning the weak and strong points of the two viewpoints. The traditionalists are at their strongest when they stress what it is that women have in common, and which at the same time distinguishes them from men, namely, "the biological rockbottom of sexual differentiation."[9] On the other hand, this position is at its weakest when it attempts to deal with the different capacities and talents of individual women. Such differences are almost as much of an embarrassment to the traditionalists as the capacity for motherhood is to the feminists.

What are the similarities between the sexes? For these are what give women's drive for equality a realistic basis,

---

American Anachronism—The Recent Image of Women and Work," Summer, 1964, by Ellen and Kenneth Keniston, refers to its "able advocacy of androgyny."

[8] *Ibid.*, pp. 633–634.

[9] Erik H. Erikson, "Inner and Outer Space: Reflections on Womanhood," in *Daedalus*, Spring, 1964, p. 598.

and it is difficult to regard them as mere feminist propaganda. The facts of similarity are not in dispute, actually, in the feminist-traditionalist argument, only what stress or interpretation is to be given them.

Dorothy Dohen has given us a very precise insight into the matter of similarity when she observed that "women differ more widely among themselves than they differ as a group compared with men."[10] Leaving aside for the moment the primary sexual difference—admittedly, this is a large exception—extreme dissimilarities come within and not across sex lines.[11] Tests such as the College Board Examination can throw only a little light on similarities and differences of the sexes. If, for example, one reads that girls do better than boys in the verbal section of the Scholastic Aptitude Test, the immediate impression is likely to be that there is a rather sharp difference here between the sexes: girls are "good at one kind of thing," boys at another. Actually, however, the findings given indicate differences in the average ratings of large groups, and an analysis of the figures shows that "Most girls are similar to boys [in scoring], with a minority in each sex creating the difference in averages."[12]

[10] Women in Wonderland, Sheed and Ward, New York, 1960, p. 39.

[11] According to the researches of Dr. John E. Anderson of the Institute of Child Development and Welfare in the University of Minnesota (as quoted in Her Infinite Variety. The American Woman as Lover, Mate & Rival, by Morton M. Hunt, Harper and Row, New York, 1962, p. 45), "for almost every psychological trait the difference between the average male and average female score is only about one-tenth as great as the range of differences among men, or among women."

[12] Komarovsky, Women in the Modern World, p. 20.

The half truths that are suggested by these comparisons usually lead to further errors. "Everyone knows" that physics is a masculine subject because boys are better at it than girls are; and "everyone" is sure that it is only the exceptional (and therefore somewhat eccentric girl) who can grasp the subject adequately. The sensible thing to do, of course, is to advise girls not to take physics, and instead to register for a course in Home Economics.[13]

When the matter of similarity is pressed further, one soon finds that in the mass of comparisons between men and women, some "overlapping" appears at every level. It may sound reasonable to say that the line between the sexes should not be blurred, but the more one investigates the matter, the more obvious it becomes: the line has been blurred from the very start.

It might be countered that, at the very least, one ought to be able to make clear-cut distinctions on the biological level. As if to drive this point home, Alexis Carrel in *Man the Unknown* confidently asserts that "woman differs profoundly from man. Every one of the cells of her body

---

[13] In fairness, one must admit that there appears to be a real difference at a higher level which is possibly more pronounced than that shown at the high-school or undergraduate level. The Russian experience, where women have had more scientific opportunities as a whole than have women in this country, seems to suggest this. Maurice Hindus in *House without a Roof* (Doubleday, New York, 1961) reports that "in science, women do not begin to approach men in distinction and achievement. They constitute about one-third of the post-graduate students in scientific and research institutes. Yet with some notable exceptions . . . they do not rise to top rank; and it is not because there is male prejudice against them. A teacher in Moscow University told me that the higher realms of science, particularly chemistry, physics, and mathematics, are too difficult for women." P. 286.

bears the mark of her sex. The same is true of her organs, and above all of her nervous system."[14]

Well, even at this level the distinction is often really a matter of proportion rather than of absolute polarity. A notable example concerns the hormones secreted by the sex glands which govern the development of sexual characteristics, voice, muscles, body hair, and so forth. Women's bodies do not produce only female hormones, and men's male hormones. On the contrary, there must be a complicated interaction of *both* male and female hormones for each sex to develop normally, although the masculine and feminine balance is different.

The clue that it is a difference in proportion rather than a clear-cut line of separation which distinguishes the sexes, seems to be valid at most levels. Men and women are not masculine or feminine because they possess an exclusive list of male or female characteristics, but because these elements, even allowing for individual differences, are not in the same balance in the two sexes.

One can, for instance, set up a series of opposing traits that are characteristically "masculine" or "feminine." For masculinity these might include activity, independence, domineeringness, adventurousness, logic; and for feminine counterparts passivity, dependency, submissivenes, shyness, and intuition.[15] But a normally feminine woman would not possess the second list at full strength with no mixture of the qualities in the first. If she were really "all woman," the results would be something less than ideal.

With so many demonstrated similarities between men

[14] Harper and Brothers, New York, 1935, pp. 89–90.
[15] This is a partial list taken from *The Road to Emotional Maturity* by David Abrahamsen, M.D., Prentice-Hall, Englewood Cliffs, 1958, p. 149.

and women, so much "overlapping" of sex-linked characteristics, what does it really mean to say that there is a "profound" difference between the two sexes? Is it the rather marked distinction between the tastes and interests of men and women that any casual observer notes at a glance? The well-known Terman-Miles Masculinity-Femininity Index seems to give very precise confirmation of the profound difference: "From whatever angle we have examined them the males included in the standardized groups evinced a distinctive interest in exploit and adventure, in outdoor and physically strenuous occupations, in machinery and tools, in science, physical phenomena, and inventions; and, from rather occasional evidence, in business and commerce. On the other hand, the females of our groups have evinced a distinctive interest in domestic affairs and in aesthetic objects and occupations; they have distinctly preferred more sedentary and indoor occupations, and occupations more directly administrative, particularly to the young, the helpless, the distressed."[16]

The notion that this sort of evidence proves that there is a profound cleavage between the sexes becomes, however, less credible on a closer look. First of all, it does not take into account the sort of general level of group interest that one can observe on its most elementary level, for example, at a party. Although the men may gather at one of the room and talk about sports and jobs, and the women at the other end and discuss children and casseroles, there is certainly more than one desperately bored individual in each group. In the tests themselves, moreover, as is the case with

[16] L. M. Terman and Catherine C. Miles, *Sex and Personality. Studies in Masculinity and Femininity*, McGraw-Hill, New York, 1936, pp. 447–448.

the College Board scores, the scorings are averages, not of individual men and women. On the individual level, where we have jockeys who collect *objets d'art* and women who scream themselves hoarse at a baseball game, the "overlapping" reasserts itself.

Even less certain in this Gargantuan area of male-female interest, is whether particular choices indicate basic nature, or simply cultural prodding and conditioning. The chances of proving the matter decisively one way or the other are not at all good. Do little girls like dolls because of the mother in them, or because dolls are what they invariably find under the Christmas tree? Is the mature woman's interest in "aesthetic objects" due to her sensitive feminine nature, or simply to the fact that she was urged to take fine-arts classes at school, while her brother was encouraged to believe that painting was for sissies? All we know is that age, education, and occupation greatly affect the degree of difference between the sexes on this kind of scale. Increased age alone makes men and women's scores resemble each other more and more.[17] Higher education, greater

[17] As to what the change with age signifies, there is sharp difference of opinion. Cervantes, for instance, attributes the age difference mainly to hormones: ". . . the interests of men are more typically male at the age of sixteen and a half . . . which is also about the time when his system produces the maximum of male hormones. Man's typical male interests likewise decline with the decline of his reproductive system." *Marriage and the Family*, p. 202. Morton Hunt, however, would disagree almost completely: ". . . the average difference between male scores and female scores for the population at large decreases with time and experience; men and women become less masculine and less feminine respectively, year by year, as their experiences wear away at the rigid sex-role definitions they began with in adolescence." *Her Infinite Majesty*, p. 42.

intelligence, a job that broadens one's interests, all diminish the differences; and the positive contrast that once seemed so clear now gradually erodes.

Obviously, the case for a profound difference between the sexes must rest on solider ground than an M-F scale. The real basis of difference is the fact that human beings inevitably experience life through the medium of a body, and that body, for the normal person, is quite definitely male or female. Needless to say, this is not a novel or startling viewpoint. One runs the risk, moreover, of appearing to pile platitude on platitude when one adds that the difference between experiencing life through a woman's body and a man's is that one is organized for motherhood and the other is not. Nevertheless, banal as its observation may seem, the difference is there, and to confine its influence firmly to the "biological level" is to take a rather superficial view of the relationship of mind and body.

Fundamental though this difference is, it is not one that is easily put into words. An accumulation of facts about the physiology of women really conveys very little to a woman who is trying to understand her own nature, and such an accumulation explains perhaps even less to a man. One may demonstrate, for instance, that the woman is fundamentally hardier than the man, less subject to serious diseases, and generally longer lived. One may also go on to show that this is really biological superiority, linked to sex, and not a matter of environment.[18] One might, further-

18 "The life expectancy for newborn girls is about 6.3 years longer than that for boys in the United States. . . . It is often argued that woman is a parasite who lives on man, and that he dies sooner because he is worn out by his daily exertions on her behalf. But Father Francis Madigan and Professor Rupert B. Vance of the

more, supplement this picture of basic hardiness with a long list of all the physical discomforts and unpleasant symptoms to which woman allegedly becomes subject merely by being female. The gamut runs from being more prone to "flushing, fainting, and various glandular disturbances"[19] to the "relentless periodicity of . . . menstrual cycles"[20] and all the annoying possibilities of pre-menstrual tension that may accompany the cycle, ranging from swollen ankles to accident-proneness. If one adds to this every possible side-effect of pregnancy, as well as the "progressive physical incapacitation of pregnancy and delivery,"[21] one has succeeded in drawing a formidable but possibly misleading picture.

What we are given to believe in, in effect, is an almost irritatingly viable creature, who pays for her long life by being very much at the mercy of her own body. Granted that women are aware of the fluctuating weather of their own bodies and of the statistical probability that they will be widows, does any of this really convey what it means to be a woman rather than a man? The chances are that the sum of this information tends to depress rather than enlighten. The piling up of clinical detail, for instance, on the discomforts, "incapacitations," and possible dangers of pregnancy, is to overlook the deeper meaning which

---

University of North Carolina recently gathered the life records of some 42,000 Catholic Brothers and Sisters, whose ways of life are practically identical . . . the Brothers lived longer than other men —but the Sisters lived longer than other women, and by an even greater margin." Morton Hunt, *Her Infinite Majesty*, pp. 31–32.

[19] Dohen, *Women in Wonderland*, p. 31.

[20] Cervantes, *Marriage and the Family*, p. 308.

[21] *Ibid.*, p. 308.

motherhood has for most women. Perhaps the majority of people, Dr. Esther Harding has suggested, "overestimate the sufferings of motherhood, not realizing that this is woman's share in the discipline of life which is as necessary for her spiritual well-being as work is for a man's."[22]

Nor does Freudian theory cast much light on what it means to be a woman. Freud's expression that anatomy is destiny promises revelation, but the revelation which unfolds tells us more about neurotic conflicts than about a complete theory of feminine development.[23] Is it not somewhat arbitrary to single out a rankling sense of organic inferiority as the basis of femininity, when a positive explanation also exists? Girls are likely to become rather aware early in life that being a woman promises motherhood, and it seems reasonable to suppose that this knowledge would give them a sense of themselves as having a special capacity, and not just as lacking something. Psychoanalyst Erik Erikson has expressed this as the sense of having a *productive inner-bodily space* safely set in the center of female form and carriage," and finds confirmation of this concept in his observations of children's typical play constructions.[24]

This may all sound rather vague and metaphorical in contrast to data about X and Y chromosomes and the details of feminine physiology. Nevertheless, it seems a good

[22] *The Way of All Women*, David McKay, New York, 1933, p. 192.

[23] Freud's theory of "genital trauma" has been criticized by various psychiatrists, both Freudian and those of other schools: Karen Horney, Clara Thomas, Gregory Zilboorg.

[24] "Inner and Outer Space," p. 587. See also his *Childhood and Society*, Norton, New York, 1963, pp. 97–108.

deal more expressive of the way in which a person "feels" herself to be womanly rather than manly. This feeling of "vital inner potential"[25] is something which has to be taken seriously into account in any theorizing about the nature of woman. Both in its presence and in its experienced absence, as the fear of being left empty,[26] the notion of "inner space" casts real light on the way in which women experience themselves and attempt to build their lives.[27]

One final point should be made about the "biological rockbottom" of woman's nature. A great deal of what is said about the female body's being built or organized for motherhood could also be said about any higher animal. One suspects that it is this implication which makes some women rather resentful of any discussion that remains on the biological level. Their whole function in life seems to be defined in a suspiciously "mammalian" fashion. Therefore, it seems worth-while to emphasize, as have recent participants on the debate on contraception, that even on a strictly biological level, women are *not* just like other higher animals.

Two very striking differences can be pointed out. The first is that a woman's sexual receptiveness is not as directly linked to reproduction in women as it is in other animals. It is not linked to seasonal or cyclical modifications in

[25] Erikson, "Inner and Outer Space," p. 594.

[26] *Ibid.* In *Childhood and Society* he remarks that the "fear of being left empty . . . seems to be the basic feminine fear." P. 410.

[27] It would seem reasonable to assume that this "experience of the ground-plan of the human body" for the girl or for the woman who has not actually experienced motherhood is not so much an actual "experiencing" of her own body as a self-appropriation of the fact that this is the way women's bodies are made.

physiology, but, on the contrary, fulfills both a relational and a procreational role. In this respect, being "female" seems to be less directly tied into motherhood for a human than for the other species.

In the second difference, that woman's life span greatly exceeds her reproductive span, there seems to be an even more marked contrast. Women differ in their sexual-life pattern from men in this respect, that men can continue to be fathers even into their eighties and nineties, while with women, menopause causes a sharp and decisive end to reproduction capability. But with higher animals, for example female monkeys and apes, there is no such break. When their reproductive life is over, life itself comes to an end.[28] It is manifestly incorrect, however, even in discussions on the biological level, to suggest that interpretation of woman's nature must center on her capacity of motherhood. A female primate is truly bound to this function down to the last days of her life; a woman, even in her basic capacity for reproduction, is not.

A summary of this kind can only begin to skim over the mass of evidence which is accumulating on the nature of woman, but even so brief a survey raises the question of whether or not all these facts and insights can be gathered together in a single theory of feminine nature. Perhaps still

[28] "No adult female monkey or ape has ever been observed who was too old to go through the oestrus cycle and reproduce." Phyllis C. Jay, "The Female Primate," in The Potential of Women, edited by Seymour M. Farber and Roger H. L. Wilson, McGraw-Hill, New York, 1963, p. 11. In the same volume, in an article entitled "The Biological Make-Up of Women," Edmund W. Overstreet comments that rarely "is there found among the higher animals in nature a female surviving much beyond the age of reproductive life." P. 22.

more to the point would be the question: What relevance would this general theory have to the struggle of the individual woman to understand herself and her own particular vocation?

Certainly, any realistic theory about women would have to avoid past errors which exaggerated similarities between the sexes into identity, or differences into opposition. It would have to hold two relevant sets of facts in balance, and not simply minimize one or the other. The first is the body of knowledge that we have about "overlapping," the indications that on various levels a woman (or a man) constitutes a blend of feminine and masculine elements or characteristics, and that what constitutes femininity is a balance in which the feminine predominates. The other significant information is on the so-called "biological rock-bottom" and its most notable consequence, motherhood. We might sum up the two by saying that there is nothing about a female physicist which goes against "feminine nature," but that it would be rather unsettling to find a male physicist who was pregnant.

But the second question raised of the whole relevance of theories of femininity to the particular woman is critical, as it is in this respect, above all, that past theories of feminine nature have been deficient. The traditional view, in emphasizing motherhood as the key to understanding women, simply levels out any individual differences. Presumably, the "natural" mother who raises a large family with competence and joy, and a quite different sort of woman who is better at handling mathematical calculations than babies, are both equally fulfilled in a wholly domestic role. In fact, all the particular talents which do not fit easily into a "nurturing" concept of woman, not to mention the long years in a modern woman's life when the bearing and raising of children is over, are left unaccounted for, perplexingly useless gifts of God. The feminist view, by contrast, seems at first to favor the individual, but in reality it favors only a particular sort of individual, the woman who is best fitted to compete in a man's world in a man's way. Those who are less equipped for such competition, less determined, or simply unwilling to devalue one side of their nature in the service of another, are seen as negligible.

It is, therefore, most important, in any fresh theorizing, to begin with a solid respect for the complexity and the uniqueness of the individual. There should be a good deal less concern for Woman, impressive and anonymous, and more for the separate and rather unpredictable personalities that make up half the human race. It would be well to hold firmly in mind that, in spite of statistics, the average woman does not exist.[29] Even better might be a temporary moratorium on the advice to women to be true to their feminine nature. A practical and even spiritual replacement might be found in Virginia Woolf's exhortation to women that "it is much more imporant to be oneself than anything else."[30]

How is it, one wonders, that the first advice, on the receiving end at least, seems so peculiarly useless? Perhaps

[29] Gordon W. Allport, *Pattern and Growth in Personality*, Holt, Rinehart, and Winston, New York, 1961, remarks that it "is certainly safe to say that no one is average in all his endocrine, anatomical, neural, cortical, and motivational capacities." P. 7.

[30] *A Room of One's Own*, Harcourt, Brace, New York, 1929, p. 193.

the simplest reason is that one's fundamental sexual being, however profoundly rooted it may be, is normally quite unself-conscious. One is no more concerned with staying feminine in the course of day-to-day life than one is with staying right-handed.

We might even use this as an analogy and say that being a woman is something like being right-handed. The left hand might correspond to the masculine elements in one's personality, the right to the dominant feminine elements. Obviously, one does not ordinarily go about one's business deeply intent on being right-handed, and quite determined not to make use of the left hand. The dominant use of one hand rather than the other is perfectly natural and unself-conscious—as is the frequent and cooperative use of the left hand. Such consciousness as there might be is simply the awareness of having hands, and of using those hands as effectively as possible.

Asking a woman to be true to herself, then, is not the same thing as urging her to be feminine. Truth to herself will necessarily include many of the traits and values which we label as feminine, and a respect for that basic ground-plan of the body which God has given to woman. But genuine fidelity to oneself must mean fidelity to the particular idea that God wished to express by creating a person, an idea whose richness and singularity cannot be expressed simply in terms of femininity. Here, once again, lies a key to a more positive concept of woman's nature in a God-centered respect for individuality, for difference, for many-sidedness. We are dealing, after all, with the endless possibilities of the "quite possible She."

III

Woman's Place

On the face of it, "being oneself" in marriage would seem to be more complicated than fidelity to self in single life. Not infrequently, the way out of this dilemma for the feminine "individualist" has been to remain single. To be a "career woman," for instance, has most often meant to be unmarried, or, if married, childless;[1] and the exceptions, at least in this country, have not been very numerous.[2] Even the choice of higher education a few decades ago, when this was still a relatively unusual course, meant that one impressively increased one's chances of remaining unmarried.[3]

[1] An extensive survey of college graduates (*They Went to College* by Ernest Havemann and Patricia Salter West, Harcourt Brace, New York, 1952) in the late 1940's indicated that working wives among the graduates were not likely to have children: "If the Former Coed decides to spend a year or so as a working wife, the chances are pretty good that she will remain a jobholder forever, and will never have children." P. 88.

[2] They have been rare enough for Betty Friedan in *The Feminine Mystique* to refer to them as " 'mutations,' the image of what the American woman can be." P. 375.

[3] The Havemann and West figures for women over 50 showed 35 per cent of the graduates unmarried as compared to 8 per cent in the general population. *They Went to College*, pp. 62–63.

If we turn to the traditional Christian view of women, we find that it, too, has dealt with individuality mainly in relation to the single woman. Certainly, the Church has never subscribed to the view, strongly promoted by some secular anti-feminists, that all normal women can and should find full expression of their gifts in marriage and motherhood. By holding out the religious life as a possibility, Christian tradition has honored an almost feminist independence. Pope Pius XII opened out further possibilities by speaking of single life in the world as another form of Christian vocation, even if it were one seemingly imposed by circumstance rather than by choice. With a sensitive recognition of the needs and potentialities of single laywomen, he pointed out that ". . . their mission at the present day is revealed: a mission many-sided, militant, and calling for all their energies; a mission such as they can more readily undertake than many of their sisters, occupied as they are with family cares and the education of their children, or else subject to the yoke of a religious rule."[4]

In both of these roles there is ample scope for a fidelity to one's individual gifts. But it must be said that the envisioned individuality is not compatible with marriage and motherhood.

If the choice between a mission to the world and a vocation to motherhood has been rather clear-cut in the past, it is because when married women rarely outlived their child-bearing years or were fully occupied with work in the home, there was little range for the fulfillment of their personality. The perplexities of combining one sort

[4] Address to Italian Women, October 21, 1945.

of fidelity to oneself with another scarcely existed. Indeed, there is little to infer from past attitudes that with recognition of the far-reaching changes in the lives of married women there will be no reëxamination of what the role and proper sphere of action for the wife and mother might be.

Already there are some indications of change. One instance would be the progressive recognition by recent popes of the place of women—including married women —in public life. Moreover, one certainly gets an impression of a fresh viewpoint within the Church in the remarks of Cardinal Suenens on the modern woman which we cited in our first chapter, with his attention to her increased leisure, her "extra life" when her children have grown, and "the atmosphere that allows her to make use of her natural gifts."[5] But oddly enough, Cardinal Suenens then goes on to chart out a program for the modern nun, not the modern housewife. Although a sociologist like Father John L. Thomas may point out that the traditional view that "woman's place is in the home" is now only a "half truth,"[6] he provides no specifications for her new role and "place." The Christian laywoman who wishes to discover what true fidelity to herself in marriage might mean will find no blueprints readily available. Apart from such clerical encouragements as we have indicated and a useful set of limitations for her speculations, she has little to guide her.

She might begin the exploration of her role in marriage

[5] *The Nun in the World*, pp. 11–12.
[6] *The American Catholic Family*, Prentice-Hall, Englewood Cliffs, 1956, pp. 353–354.

by studying the historical development of the Christian view of her role as wife and mother; but there is a less orthodox approach which might make a more useful point of departure. If she wishes to see both the strengths and the weaknesses of the traditional concept of her role, there is no better way than a careful look at recent neo-femininst approaches to the woman's role in marriage. Such a look will be more useful than it might have been in the past, as these secularist views now tend to deal explicitly with self-fulfillment in married life rather than centering on the single career woman.

It is becoming increasingly obvious, in other words, that the "middle-ground" approach to the married woman's role has meant that the present-day feminist is likely to find a husband and a carefully controlled number of children manageable, and even desirable additions to her scheme of life. The point of such a book as *The Feminine Mystique* was not that women should cast off the chains of marriage and motherhood, but that they could combine a family with a full use of their talents in the working world. The ideal of the career woman is changing to the "career wife"—though certainly not in the sense of the clergyman's dictum that "a woman's full-time career is usually marriage and motherhood."[7]

The cornerstone of the new feminist view of marriage is the notion that the near identity of the nature of man and woman means equivalent or nearly identical roles in marriage. The theory of virtual identity of the sexes, rather than being distorted by marriage, should be applied scrupulously to the roles of husband and wife, with as near an

[7] Cervantes, *Marriage and the Family*, p. 265.

approximation to perfect equality and "share and share alike" as possible. Needless to say, a really even-handed sharing out of the tasks of married life presents a real challenge. (No one has yet solved the problem of sharing pregnancies.) But, granted some obstinate exceptions, there is a general feeling that with proper education and the right frame of mind, most other details can be managed.

The right frame of mind is particularly important as far as the husband is concerned, for "equality of the sexes" means equality in taking on such housework and child care as cannot be delegated to paid help. This may require some adjustment on his part. As Alice Rossi remarks crisply in speaking of the partners in this type of marriage, "If her children are not to suffer from "paternal deprivation," her husband will also anticipate that the assumption of parenthood will involve a weeding out of nonessential activities either in work, civic, or social participation."[8] She is aware that this notion of marriage roles is somewhat novel and quite a contrast to earlier feminist expectations that women would move closer to the masculine standard, but that men would undergo little change; for this new "definition of sex equality stresses the enlargement of the common ground on which men and women base their lives together by changing the social definitions of approved characteristics for both sexes."[9] Nevertheless, she feels that the right sort of home training and education for boys and girls should produce the desired result of "parental substitutability" and full equality in the course of time. For example, girls would no longer be directed into classes such

[8] Rossi, "Equality between the Sexes," p. 649.
[9] Ibid., p. 608.

as cooking and child care, and boys into crafts and shop, but both would attend the same classes together, and acquire similar skills.

The point that this theory of parental equivalence is trying to make is not that fathers should play a larger part in the rearing of their children, and mothers a somewhat lesser part than has been customary in recent years. Such a point would be compatible with a quite traditional view of marriage, as there is good reason to believe that the present proportions of time and energy invested in, and influence over child-rearing are somewhat out of line for both sexes. What is really being stated here is that *both* parents can and should shift their center of gravity outside the family, and, for practical reasons, as well as to avoid the dangers of "parental deprivation," this means that the husband may have to take on some aspects of the wife's traditional role. In effect, this means that the mother's relationship with her children will approximate the relatively independent relationship between father and child.

The even-handed reassignment of roles in marriage, even if it is not carried to quite this extreme, raises a number of questions. One of the more relevant is whether any substantial number of women—not to mention their husbands—want this sort of redistribution of roles. To put the matter somewhat differently, one wonders whether, in the absence of financial pressures, women place fulfillment in outside work ahead of staying home with their young children.

In this country, the answer for the majority of mothers has apparently been *no*. Unless her salary is urgently needed, it is the exceptional woman who returns to work

full time before her children are in school. However, the
general attitude in other societies, where women are encouraged to combine work and motherhood—at least those
who are professional women—seems to be somewhat different. There are indications that in a country like Russia,
for instance, the "maternal instinct" often runs a poor
second to an interest in work. One recent observer, who
interviewed a number of Russian mothers, reports: "Out
of close to 20 young and old women with whom I talked
at length, not one was without a profession or was not
studying for one. . . . These women were proud of their
right to work. . . . Through education they had specialties
which made it impossible to sit at home. For them, work
was an exciting challenge, taxing their best talents and
keeping them alert.[10] It would be wrong to say that these
women felt no pull to stay with their small children, but
it was a pull that was usually overcome in practice. One
young doctor who had left her children with their grandmother in the country admitted, "I was restless to go back
to my job. The day goes by, you're exhausted from housework, and you have not really done anything challenging,
constructive, or inspiring. . . . But," she added, "I die a
thousand deaths every day, I miss them so much."[11]

The *Times* report concludes: "Many Russian women
with whom I spoke were faced with this problem. They
were torn between their desire to work and realize their
own potential and their equally strong desire to spend

[10] Elena Whiteside, "On the Job and at Home: Russian Housewife's 13-Hour Day," New York *Times*, Western Edition, November 19, 1963.
[11] *Ibid.*

their time with their children. . . . Most of them choose work, leaving their children temporarily with grandparents."[12]

Two tentative conclusions might be drawn from this brief look at the Russian experience. The first is that it reinforces the feminist argument that many women are like men in having strong interests which have little to do with domestic life. But the second conclusion, that women who attempt to carry on these interests full time throughout their married life are likely to undergo a sharp internal conflict, casts doubt on the whole feminist contention that identical roles in marriage are natural and represent genuine self-fulfillment.

The somewhat more fragmentary experience with working mothers of young children in other Western countries bears out these conclusions. The impression sometimes given by defenders of the traditional view of woman's role in marriage, that women, given a choice, prefer domestic life, and are only driven to outside work by financial pressure or propaganda, is somewhat misleading. It can be applied with relative safety to women in unskilled and uninteresting work, but with educated women in more challenging jobs, the picture is different. As the authors of a study of women and work in four Western countries comment: ". . . the difference in the attitude to work is . . .

[12] Ibid. David and Vera Mace in The Soviet Family (Doubleday, Garden City, 1963) report that "Nurseries or creches for working mothers were started soon after the Revolution and were a basic element in the policy of the regime. . . . But practice has not yet been able to catch up with theory. . . . Today, the proportion provided for is rising rapidly, but it is not likely that throughout the country as a whole it would exceed 20 per cent." P. 268.

quite marked between different strata—which do not necessarily coincide with social classes. Women with higher education or a specialized training who have known the satisfactions of responsibility or of skilled work, are, naturally, more loath to give up their jobs on marrying than girls who have done semi-skilled or routine work . . . the highly skilled or the professional woman who has to give up her career for domestic routine is likely to feel frustrated after some time if she cannot use her abilities."[13] In fact, most American sociologists, observing conditions in this country, would come to similar judgments about the work attitudes of professional women, and would conclude that their motives do not differ very greatly from those of their male counterparts.

For the woman who combines a rather demanding job with a growing family, the conflict actually cuts two ways. It is not only the "strictly feminine goals" that are jeopardized. The author of one book on women executives remarks that having a husband "may even be a good busi-

[13] Alva Myrdal and Viola Klein, *Women's Two Roles—Home and Work*, Routledge & Kegan Paul, Ltd., London, 1956, pp. 9–10. This difference also seems to be borne out by the Russian experience, as reported by Maurice Hindus: "On both recent journeys to the Soviet Union, I was interested to learn whether career women whose husbands earned high enough salaries to support the family were tiring of their careers and preferred to stay at home and look after their families . . . to the best of my knowledge the percentage of those who do so is comparatively small. . . . They enjoy being useful and 'creative.'" Factory workers who "still bear the double burden as mothers and workers" feel differently, particularly as Soviet men do *not* share the housework, but they cannot afford to work: "Very few men . . . earn enough in any Soviet factory to support their families." *House without a Roof*, pp. 287–288, 185.

ness asset. . . . But a family—that's something else again."[14]

Why a family should be "something else again," something of a liability, is explained more seriously by Helene Deutsch in terms of a division of "psychic energy." Speaking of the woman who wavers between the duties of wife and mother and those of a professional career, she says: "The active woman actually does transfer to other goals psychic energies that she otherwise would spend directly on the objects of her environment, particularly on her children. And, conversely, not all her psychic energies are available for these goals, because, as a woman, she has spent them emotionally on more direct object relations."[15] Even if the woman with a demanding job can afford adequate help with the housekeeping, the often unpredictable joys and catastrophes in the lives of her small children, from measles to celebrations, drain on her time and energy in a way that she would never have known as a single woman.

Although this aspect of the conflict does exist, it is not the one usually stressed. More troublesome is the effect of a career on the relationship of mother and child. For a mother with full-time interests outside the home, the question is going to be whether she is giving enough to her children, not whether she is giving enough to her work.

Most of the ways of answering this question will strike the inquiring laywoman as rather evasive. There is, for example, the typically masculine evasion (which does not even work very well for fathers) that, in terms of the added salary, a working woman has indeed given enough. With-

[14] Frances Maule, *Executive Careers for Women*, Harper and Brothers, 1957–1961, p. 218.

[15] Helene Deutsch, M.D., *Psychology of Women*, volume one, *Girlhood*, Grune and Stratton, New York, 1944, p. 290.

out it, there would be no college education, travel, trips to the orthodontist, attractive clothes, and the rest.[16] Whether or not the child's most pressing need is two "good providers" for parents is not touched upon.

A more pretentious evasion involves shifting the question itself around. Rather than asking whether the mother is giving enough to her children, she is asked whether she is giving enough to live up to society's idea of motherhood: "The married woman with young children tries to be a conscientious mother; indeed, she seems more likely than the average to serve as a Den Mother and to attend the P.T.A. faithfully. . . . Still, the mother-wife-executive often wears a troubled expression that reflects her misgivings. However affectionate and able a mother she may be, she often worries about fulfilling society's expectations of the Mother."[17]

Another, slightly brisker commentator manages to circle around the subject to much the same end: "For the professional businesswoman, painter, musician, editor, who is also a mother, the problems are quite real and quite serious. She, unlike the single woman or the part-time profes-

---

[16] See the explanation of an "executive" mother quoted by Frances Maule, who said of her relationship to her children: " 'I'm their guarantee that they can have most of the things possessed by the other kids of their acquaintance.' " The author comments: "The reason for staying on the job most commonly advanced by working mothers is the desire to maintain—and even raise—the family standard of living, and more specifically to provide the educational and social advantages necessary to enable their children to attain and hold a place in the social and economic scale as high as or higher than their own." *Executive Careers for Women,* p. 222.

[17] Margaret Cussler, *The Woman Executive,* Harcourt, Brace, New York, 1958, pp. 42–43.

sional, needs to face the question of whether or not she can play the typical mother role. Her relationships with her children and husband can be positive and warm, but she can never create the child-centered family which has come to be the ideal today. She can be worried about her children, but the show must go on. This means that both she and her children have to learn somehow—and very early—to accept her professional status."[18]

In this case, the troubled expression might belong to a two-year-old, trying to accept his mother's "professional status" and not just to the "mother-wife-executive"; but the way of stating the problem is about the same. The mother in question is presumed to be doing her best, but is it good enough for society, with its exigent demands for "child-centered" families and a "typical mother role"?

Neither of these answers really represents the current feminist response, which is decidedly more aggressive than evasive. The conflict between home and work is triumphantly settled by assuring the working mother that her children are much better off without her—at least on a "full-time" basis. The absent mother not only provides her children with material benefits, but simply by being absent, she is providing them with the best emotional climate as well.

The first step in this argument is to prove that regular absence of the mother has no undesirable effects. Moreover, reasonably enough, the problem of regular absence has been distinguished from the sort of sudden and shocking

[18] Ethel J. Alpenfels, in *American Women. The Changing Image*, edited by Beverley Benner Cassara, Beacon Press, Boston, 1962, pp. 88–89.

separation from the mother that occurs with death or an accident, as well as from the effects of institutional care without any "mothering" of infants and small children. The genuinely damaging effects of such shock and of institutionalization have been clearly demonstrated in various studies,[19] but it does not necessarily follow that a mother's going to work would have the same results. The feminist contention is that all such inferences have proved so far to be quite unwarranted. "What effect *does* maternal employment have upon children?" Mrs. Rossi asks. "Many sociologists of the family have raised this question during the past fifteen years, expecting to find negative effects as psychoanalytic theory predicted. . . ." Her reply is that, "to date, *there is no evidence of any negative effects traceable to maternal employment;* children of working mothers are no more likely than children of non-working mothers to become delinquent, to show neurotic symptoms, to feel deprived of maternal affection, to perform poorly in school, to lead narrower social lives, etc."[20]

But this argument that the children of working mothers are no worse off than those with "full-time" mothers is not really considered adequate for the purpose. The next step is to prove that full-time mothering is quite disastrous, not merely for the frustrated would-be executive, but for the children themselves. The absent mother is sparing her children the really nasty effects of her oversolicitous pres-

[19] Anna Freud's studies of children in World War II, for example, are often cited to show the need for a mother or mother-substitute relationship in a child's normal development.

[20] "Equality between the Sexes," pp. 617–618. Betty Friedan treats this subject more extensively in Chapter 12 of *The Feminine Mystique.*

ence. Once again, we rely on Mrs. Rossi's question and answer: "Are children better off for having full-time mothers? . . . the answer . . . is a firm *no*. Educators, child psychologists and social analysts report an increasing tendency for American middle-class children to be lacking in initiative, excessively dependent on others for direction and decision, physically soft. . . . No society has as wide-spread a problem of juvenile delinquency and adolescent rebellion as ours. Alcoholism, compulsive sex-seeking, and adolescent delinquency . . . have been on the increase in the middle-class suburb in the past twenty years, and involve more women and girls than in the past. . . . In a large proportion of cases, the etiology of mental illness is linked to inadequacy in the mother-child relationship. A high proportion of psychoneurotic discharges from the army during World War II was traced to these young soldiers' overly dependent relationships to their mothers."[21] The tendency to blame full-time motherhood for everything from "the battered child-syndrome" to post-partum depression seems to be well under way.

The obvious weakness of this rather alarming argument lies in the fact that it is taking aim at one particular and rather vulnerable form of motherhood as it has existed in the small, frequently suburban, middle-class family of the last few decades. If one grants that most of these mothers have not only not worked outside the home, but have had few if any strong interests extending beyond their own families, the task of proving that this type of "full-time" mothering can be oppressive is like shooting fish in a barrel.

The basic difficulty which these mothers may face has

[21] *Ibid.*, pp. 620–621.

been expressed half-humorously: "Today, with only two children to start with, there is no margin for error. Every child must turn out well, turn out well in every respect."[22] The small family which has been the conscious choice of most of these women provides a somewhat inadequate and tension-producing field for a full-time "career" of motherhood.

Not only are two or three children a rather small number to absorb the impact of any possible failures in a woman's chosen career, but the potentialities for an anxious relationship between mother and children, in itself more likely to induce failure, have considerably increased over recent years. The educated, middle-class mother has been made painfully aware by experts of all degrees of reliability of the perils involved in child-raising. It may increase a mother's self-importance to assure her that her child is formed for life (under her nearly exclusive care) by the age of three—or possibly seven—but it is equally likely to make her extremely worried. That particular age seems to roll by all too soon, leaving with the mother the continued, but perhaps futile, responsibility for a child who may have been psychologically maimed for life by her blunders. Indeed, the possibilities for blundering are quite all-embracing, taking in every move she has or has not made in feeding, toilet-training, discipline, handling sibling rivalry, and giving affection. If her labor-saving household devices give her the time, she can sort out her errors all over again at her apprehensive leisure.

There is a further peculiarity of modern, middle-class

[22] Sidonie M. Gruenberg and Hilda Sidney Krech, *The Many Lives of Modern Woman*, Doubleday, Garden City, 1952, p. 20.

family life which has made it vulnerable, and this has been the isolation of mother and children. There are not only fewer children to absorb the mother's attention, but fewer adults to keep her company as well. With the virtual disappearance of the "extended" family and of full-time domestic servants, as well as the husband's frequent separation from the home for outside work, this isolation has become rather complete. Such a situation is not pure gain for any of those concerned: mothers have difficulty in remaining "adult" when they spend most of their time in a child's world, and children are put in the somewhat oppressive position of having to be a world, not to mention a "career," for their mothers. Concentrated, isolated, and self-conscious mothering is further reinforced by the disappearance of much productive work which was formerly done in or around the home, leaving the present-day housewife almost too free to be with her children at all times.

It is one thing, however, to suggest that children could benefit by a more relaxed relationship with their mothers, or that 'round-the-clock care by one person is not necessary, or that mothers need interests outside the home, and quite another to claim that children's lives are improved by getting the majority of their care from "mother substitutes" and day-care centers.

Anyone who studies this feminist view of motherhood must wonder why the suggested remedy should lead to a situation so far removed from the supposedly healthier mother-child relationship of an earlier period. It is undoubtedly true that the housewife of another day absorbed in sewing, planting, cooking, and cleaning, delegated more of the care of her children to others, and very probably worried less about child-raising than the contemporary suburban mother. But unlike the "wife-mother-executive" who is supposed to be her present counterpart, she was around if her children needed her. There was no need for a small child to "accept her professional status" by resigning himself to her complete absence during most of his waking hours.

It is in this "acceptance" by the child that the most striking flaw in the theory of identical parental roles in marriage lies, for what the child "accepts" is not so much the "identical" parents, the pair of good providers and spare-time companions, as it is a substitute mother or mothers. If his biological mother returns to work in a few months, someone else must be found to provide not only routine physical care, but warmth and affection; and that someone will undoubtedly be a woman. It is worth noting that in spite of the talk of "parental substitutability," there is no talk of bringing in a "practical father." Nor will the small child be turned over to a day-care center run by men. The arithmetic of identity does not quite work out. In order to achieve even the appearance of identity, another woman, the "substitute mother," must be brought into the wife-husband-child relationship.

One way of expressing the rather baffling mathematics of this situation is to say that it deals in visible additions and invisible subtractions. Self-fulfillment or "being oneself" in marriage is made to seem like a simple matter of addition. The role in marriage envisioned for the wife "will not mark a withdrawal from the life and work pattern that she has established"; rather it "will be an enlargement of her life experiences."[23] If one grants that any woman, no matter how talented, still has at her disposal only twenty-

[23] Rossi, "Equality between the Sexes," p. 649.

four hours a day and a limited amount of "psychic energy," the addition of home, husband, and children to the "life pattern" that she has established means that some sort of subtraction is going to take place. The subtraction is invisible. The "experience" of motherhood ("one among many equally important highlights in her life") still remains on the surface, but the time-consuming substance has been quietly removed.

The woman who is interested in a role in marriage which expresses a genuine fidelity to self might be rather mistrustful of this sort of sleight-of-hand. She will concede that one kind of fidelity to self has been retained. If the absentee mother as a single woman was a good artist, or scientist, or businesswoman, making the best use of her individual talents, she has indeed remained faithful to this concept of herself in marriage. There has been no subtraction here. But she has not really added to this a fidelity to that other side of herself which has found a physical expression in marriage and motherhood. On the contrary, such a fidelity, if she would even concede that it exists, has been largely delegated away. Further, if the identity to which she is faithful is not male, it is at least virginal.

Indeed, all that part of a woman's nature which has been summarized as her sense of the "ground-plan" of her body gets short shrift in the feminist view of marriage just described. If any sense of a "vital inner potential" is involved, it is certainly not her potentiality for motherhood. Children seem to be viewed as a sort of extra luxury which she allows herself. Motherhood must be "fitted into" one's basic role and purpose in life. Betty Friedan, in fact, states the matter in precisely those terms: "When society asks so little of women, every woman has to listen to her own

inner voice to find her identity in this changing world.
She must create, out of her own needs and abilities, a new
life plan, *fitting in the love and children and home* [my
italics] that have defined femininity in the past with the
work toward a greater purpose that shapes the future."[24]

In this view, bearing and raising one's children apparently have very little to do with shaping the future and still
less with finding one's own identity. On the contrary, as
"the same range of potential ability exists for women as
for men,"[25] the problem of finding their identity is precisely the same—it lies in their work outside the home:
"Women, as well as men, can only find their identity in
work that uses their full capacities. A woman cannot find
identity through others—her husband, her children. She
cannot find it in the dull routine of housework. . . . The
only way for a woman, as for a man, to find herself, to know
herself as a person, is by creative work of her own. There is
no other way."[26]

In this analysis, women are not to find ways to use their
full capacities and work creatively within the structure set
by marriage and motherhood—it is marriage and motherhood which must be adapted to the structure of one's work
life. The reason for this is very simple. The identity for
which one is searching can only be reached through "a
serious professional commitment" to some line of work in
the world, a "lifelong commitment to an art or science, to
politics or profession."[27] Because achievement in this work
is so critical for one's identity, it cannot, any more than it

[24] *The Feminine Mystique,* p. 338.
[25] *Ibid.,* p. 336.
[26] *Ibid.,* p. 336.
[27] *Ibid.,* p. 348.

could for a man, be put on a part-time or dilettante level. Marriage and motherhood may slightly postpone the attainment of one's goals, as a tour of compulsory military service would for a man, but it must not threaten the full achievement of the goals themselves. The sign that one has found one's identity does not lie in any inner or private assurance, but in the recognition of one's professional status by society.[28]

This view of the married woman's role is intended to solve for her what is frequently referred to as her "identity crisis" or the problem of growing up and choosing her identity. Such a decision will mean, as Erikson explains it, "the creation of a sense of sameness, a unity of personality now felt by the individual and recognized by others as having consistency in time—of being, as it were, an irreversible historical fact."[29] As the problem is frequently stated in terms of finding one's own "occupational identity," it seems to be neatly solved by selecting one's "serious professional commitment" to some line of work in the world.

Unfortunately for the married woman, this may lead quite literally to a case of "mistaken identity." It is interesting that Erikson, who is cited by Mrs. Friedan with such assurance, is careful to point out that the formation of identity for men and women cannot be presumed to be the same. Rather, he asks if a woman's sense of her identity would not necessarily differ from a man's "by dint of the fact that her somatic design harbors an 'inner space' des-

[28] Ibid., p. 349.
[29] "Youth: Fidelity and Diversity," in Daedalus, Winter, 1962, p. 15.

tined to bear . . . offspring . . . and, with it, a biological, psychological, and ethical commitment to take care of human infancy."[30] Moreover, fidelity, "the strength of disciplined devotion,"[31] and a critical virtue in working out one's occupational role, takes on a different coloring for women in view of this commitment.

We have arrived back, then, after this detour to examine "identical" roles in marriage, at a view of the woman's role which is equal in being "uniquely creative"[32]—not in being the same. Such a view, in fact, seems to develop quite naturally from our concept of feminine nature. We have suggested there that without denying that men and women share a common humanity and "overlap" in many of their traits and capacities, there is both a difference in the balance of masculine and feminine elements in each sex, and a wholly different "ground-plan" of the body oriented towards the difference in parenthood. In this light, it should already be clear that a woman's "being herself" in marriage could not be resolved by duplicating her husband's role, with a maternity leave or two as a concession to the unimportant biological differences.

If we turn from the ambiguities of "identical" parents to the long-accepted Christian picture of marriage roles, we get a first impression of reassuring if somewhat exasperating solidity. The family is a small society, hierarchical in its arrangement, whose fundamental purpose is perfectly clear: the service of new life, or, to put it more formally, the procreation and education of children. In this service,

[30] "Inner and Outer Space," p. 586.
[31] Erikson, "Youth," p. 23.
[32] *Idem,* "Inner and Outer Space," p. 605.

the division of labor between the two parents is apparently quite distinct, with no shadows of "substitutability." The father is head and protector of the family, both final authority and provider, and the mother is "heart," entrusted with the day-to-day care of the family and with building up the sense of community and relationship between its members which only one who "cares with continuity" can bring.

Perhaps the chief difficulty with this picture is that it too often seems intended to convey the impression that no significant changes have taken place in marriage roles and the quality of family life not only since the nineteenth century, but back to Adam and Eve. The clear division of roles between provider or "breadwinner" and homemaker, to take an example, would have had little relevance in the pre-industrial situation when the whole family was a productive unit.

Quite apart from the question of work in or out of the home, however, there are at least three areas in which this "unchanging" pattern of Christian marriage roles is in fact undergoing significant change, namely, in the importance placed on companionship and a genuine sharing of life, in a new understanding of the husband's authority, and in the responsibility of husband and wife to a larger community than their own family.

Of all these, the emphasis on companionship is probably the most widespread and generally accepted. Modern Western marriages, Christian and non-Christian, are no longer made as economic partnerships, nor, primarily, in order to have children, but out of love, and the hope for a total personal communion. Today's bachelor does not need a wife to sew buttons on his shirts or cook his dinner, and the working girl does not need financial support. What they do look for, in an era when people tend to become interchangeable parts, is a lasting relationship, a community of love. The fact that this widespread expectation exists is in itself both the result of and a testimony to the fundamental growth in consciousness of women and the sense of themselves as persons. In this regard, feminism, which contributed to this development, has added more to the possibilities of marriage than the assertion of a somewhat bleak androgyny. Indeed, Dr. Esther Harding has asserted that the whole underlying significance of the "woman movement" was that it brought about the sort of change in women themselves which made possible a real relationship between the sexes in which "a certain separateness is necessary."[33]

One far-reaching consequence of this change has been a deepened understanding of the purpose of marriage. It no longer seems as easy to distinguish between the "primary" and "secondary" ends of marriage and to state without qualification that the purpose of marriage is the service of new life. Certainly, the spiritual significance of this companionship has been increasingly stressed, and it is coming to be seen more clearly that the two "ends" of marriage are deeply, inextricably related. Just as fruitfulness or new life is the natural outcome of the particular sort of community of love which marriage constitutes, so is a profound and loving relationship between the parents the necessary context for the true growth of this new life. Once the "primary" end is seen not as a biological process, but as procreation and education, a long and complex business cov-

[33] The Way of All Women, pp. 95–97.

ering many years, then it becomes clear that it is only in achieving a union of life at many levels, sexual, intellectual, spiritual, that the parents can carry through the primary end by making a "matrix of personhood"[34] for their children.

It is very difficult to talk about this relationship without touching on the second area of change, the authority of the husband, and its corollary, wifely obedience. In marriage, is there an exchange of views, a sense of coresponsibility between two persons of equal dignity, or is there a sort of chain of command, with the wife occupying an uneasy position slightly above the eldest child, with the family dog at the bottom of the pyramid?

Certainly, the meaning of the husband's "headship" is no longer as obvious on a natural level as it once appeared to be. A natural and inherent superiority of man over woman is not the foundation for authority in marriage, but in an earlier period, with higher education and a wide range of occupational opportunities and experience limited to men only, this would not have been so clear. In fact, there is not a little similarity in the situation with regard to the authority of the husband and the change in authority of the parish priest over his people. Neither one is necessarily buttressed in our times by an obvious superiority of education and culture. Authority remains, but it has been

[34] "The home, in this spiritual sense, is the matrix of personhood. . . . Marriage is a bond between two people capable of supplying the human context in which the children born to them may be joined to their parents in love. A proper notion of procreation demands that we understand marriage in terms of interpersonal relationship." Gregory Baum, O.S.A., "Can the Church Change Her Position on Birth Control?" in Contraception and Holiness, Herder and Herder, New York, 1964, pp. 335–336.

stripped to a new purity of essentials. In married life, the essential element in the situation seems to be the need for an unshakable unity in family authority, which can only be assured by God's placing final responsibility for family decisions in the hands of one person, the husband, who normally is also chief guardian and provider of the whole family. Just as the love between the two parents is a vital part of the "matrix of personhood" in which children can come to their full development, so too is this unity. Love is the first essential, but even when love is present, children are inevitably damaged by two equal and divided "authorities" each going a separate way.

A free and honest exchange of opinion is at the heart of the sort of relationship which is a total communion of love. Moreover, nothing less should be expected in the type of subordination which is supposed to exist in marriage, for obedience does not "imply that the wife should be put on a level with those persons who in law are called minors, to whom it is not customary to allow free exercise of their rights because of their lack of mature judgment, or of their ignorance of human affairs."[35]

It is still more appropriate to stress coresponsibility in speaking of married obedience, rather than the supposed need of the wife for a reassuring and ever-present masculine authority. If the latter is what women need, then they are peculiarly unfortunate, since most women can only cultivate dependency on a very limited and part-time basis, given the work patterns of their husbands. The patriarchal figure on whom the family can confidently depend is not only apt to be out of the home for most of the children's

[35] Pius XI in *Casti Connubii*.

waking hours. If he is in military service, or in one of the increasing number of businesses in which he must travel regularly or make frequent trips, he may be away for days, weeks, and even months at a time. Under these conditions, the loyalty to the common good of the family which at other times might exact obedience would demand a good measure of personal initiative and coresponsibility from the wife, regardless of how much or how little she might personally wish to exercise it. Indeed, it seems to be on this loyalty, rather than on any natural tendency to dispense or depend on authority, that a genuine understanding of the headship of the husband and obedience of the wife must be based.

Just as significant as these areas of change in roles within the family "cell" is the increasingly urgent question of the relation of the husband's and wife's roles to a wider community. In fact, it is particularly important not to think of the "cell" of the family as if it had impermeable walls; or to put it somewhat differently, as if it were a fortress, a last stronghold of Christian living, whose relationship to society was purely, and indeed belligerently defensive. Simply by being both "lay" and Christian, both husband and wife should have a wholly different orientation towards the society in which they live, a specific commitment to the christianization of that society, to the "consecration of the world."

For a man, this means that he will seek primarily a kind of work that will genuinely contribute to the building up of a society based on love and justice, and so far as he has a choice, avoid any job that reduces him to a mere provider and bill-payer. Ordinarily, a full use of his talents is going to mean a sustained effort, continued and developed over many years, demanding long hours and devotion. Such work will also have to provide the necessities of life for his family, but certainly this is not the whole meaning of his work for him. Nor, for that matter, does wage-earning begin to encompass his relationship to his family.

For a married woman, there is no less commitment to the shaping of a Christian society, but the form which it takes is necessarily somewhat different. For many years, at least, her field of action is mainly within, his mainly outside, the home. A genuine and primary commitment to family life does not necessarily imply a life-long career of child-raising; but commitment does mean, for the married woman, that the life in which she creates the very basis of her children's identity comes first. It is not something merely to be "fitted in."

No doubt, in spite of the allure of "careerism," most Christian married women accept this view of their "indirect"[36] responsibility to society. In many cases, they may also envisage, however mistily, the possibility of using their talents outside the home at a later period in life. But with this, the whole question of any further social responsibility is often closed. The next generation, then, narrows down to one's own children and perhaps those of a few suitable families in the neighborhood, because one's own children "need" friends. Nor does it always seem to be grasped that even the indirect contribution cannot be made properly if it is divorced from an intense concern with the rest of the

[36] Gertrud von le Fort has said that "it belongs to the meaning of the mother that she transmit man's history-making capabilities into a given generation . . ." *The Eternal Woman*, Bruce, Milwaukee, 1954, p. 26.

human race. One cannot "transmit" love of neighbor to a child unless one has neighbors.

With marriage, and particularly with the birth of children, young women may rather abruptly shed not only specific activities for the community, but the whole attitude of concern that presumably accompanied them. Work for the world beyond one's family is suddenly taken to be man's work—or perhaps appropriate for single or older women. Admittedly, there have been certain intrusions into this state of social unconsciousness. Twenty years ago, Pius XII stated plainly that in regard to public life, "every woman without exception is under an obligation—a strict obligation of conscience—not to remain aloof." He went on to say of the Catholic woman that "it is for her to work with man for the welfare of the *civitas* in which she enjoys a dignity equal with his."[37] Unfortunately, however, these remarks were made in an address to Italian women—rather than in a well-publicized encyclical—which has made them somewhat easier to ignore. There have been intelligent programs designed to inform and activate the rank and file of Catholic women, such as those of the N.C.C.W. on Latin America and Racial Discrimination. But good as these efforts are, they will have maximum impact mainly among older women who have the time and the inclination to join organizations and attend meetings.

To be realistic, not very much change can be expected from random verbal proddings which mainly reach those who need them least. What one gets, at best, among those women who are truly involved only with their own families, is a sort of localized response. They will respond to nudges

[37] Address to Italian Women, October 21, 1945.

towards community responsibility by conscientiously voting
in the primaries and not just in the general elections, or by
soliciting for United Crusade, or serving on the neighborhood Girl Scout troop committee. Such activities barely
ripple the surface of their basic concerns. The fundamental
individualism or family isolationism remains entrenched.
Just how firmly it is entrenched is shockingly revealed by
the violence with which women will spring into political
or "community" activity when the welfare of their own
particular families seems to be directly threatened—for
example, by a change in racial residential or schooling patterns.[38]

Many of the critical, seemingly uncontrollable problems
of our society, urban blight and suburban withdrawal, radical inequalities in our public education, with its satellite
problem of drop-outs and unemployables, hinge not so
much on governmental interference or inadequacies as on
the closed cell of the family within the tightly segregated
residential neighborhood. Without the willingness of many
families to undertake personally some of the burdens of
change, its liabilities, it is difficult to see how a humanly
tolerable, let alone a "Great Society" can be built up in this
country.

Clearly, then, the married woman's role cannot be split
neatly between work in the home and work for the world

[38] The following item in the October 9, 1964, issue of the San
Francisco *Examiner*: "Fifty white mothers tried to storm police lines
yesterday outside an elementary school in a protest against classroom
integration plans. . . . For the fourth straight day pickets showed up
outside P.S. 149 in the Jackson Heights section of Queens, where 65
white parents were arrested Wednesday in a demonstration which
touched off a wild melee with police."

at large. There is no sharp line between "domestic" and "outside" activities. The very choice of a home and neighborhood, the decision to move or stay, the involvement or withdrawal from one's immediate neighbors, the guests who are welcomed, the taking into the family of a foster or adopted child, can all be, in a true sense, work for the world, for the christianization of society. During the years when their children are growing up, wives rather than husbands are the most deeply involved in the living out of these choices. The loss, if they see this area as unimportant, or significant only in giving their children a boost towards status and a higher standard of living, is incalculable. It undercuts their indirect contribution to society in trying to raise responsible children, and it opens up the possibility that "direct" contributions in later years may turn out to be refined self-aggrandizement.

The feminist view of the changes in a single woman's life when she marries might suggest a spatial image of "adding on" to a home. The house of one's identity gets a new wing "husband, home, and children." A more realistic image of what happens to a woman in marriage would be of a rather drastic remodeling from roof to cellar. Marriage will certainly mean "adding on," but it will bring transformations and diminishments as well. Some rooms will be quite unrecognizable, and others will disappear entirely.

It should not be forgotten that what is given in marriage is oneself—not some presumably more ideal wife and mother, nor a collection of services from cooking to cohabitation. It is this unique and particular person, no other, who has been chosen by one's partner for a total sharing

of life and "coresponsibility" in the raising of a family.
Beyond this, it will not just be the structure of family
responsibilities that will condition any "direct" contribution to society, nor some abstract notion of woman's contribution to the world, but one's own particular gifts and
liabilities. A woman's identity in single life, then, however
unusual a structure, is not supposed to be razed to the
ground in order to make way for a sort of tract home
version of the good wife and mother. Whatever was genuine and solid in the old structure should find its place
somewhere in the new. If being poet or teacher, nurse or
painter or scholar, was genuinely part of this self given in
marriage, then a woman is not meant to offer this part of
her self in a holocaust to the service of family life, but rather
reshape and transform it.

Transformation of this kind involves time. Spatial images
fail us, for it is time which is the critical element in dis-
cussing the role of the Christian married woman in our
society, and no approach which evades the changing pattern of a woman's life cycle by offering a static disposition
of her place and identity in marriage can be successful.
Almost inevitably, it makes possible the particularly unfortunate avoidance of any discussion of a change in that
role in middle age. Any suggestions about the opportunities which change offers her, whether modest or visionary,
must be clearly related to the problems which time poses
for her.

IV

The Discontinuous Life

When we come to consider the element of time in a married woman's life, we find that there are two words for the dilemmas which times poses for her that crop up with impressive frequency. They are "distraction" and "discontinuity." They are actually different in meaning only by degree. "Distraction" is more characteristic of the day-to-day life of the housewife and mother, but when it comes to long periods of time, years and not hours and days, the designatory word is "discontinuity."

To say that a woman's life is discontinuous in one sense means simply that there are rather sharp breaks between one stage of a woman's life and the next. A more significant meaning which has only recently come to the fore, however, is that there is no real cohesion, no over-all pattern tying together the different stages of her existence.

Undoubtedly, breaks or sharply marked transitions have always been more characteristic of a woman's typical life cycle than of a man's. They are the extension in time of the basic ground-plan of her body, of her basic rhythm as a woman. This is not to say that there is no cohesiveness at all to the pattern of a woman's life. On the contrary, this rhythm provides a sort of built-in cohesiveness and continuity, that is, if one assumes, as so many generations and societies have, that a woman's main function in life is motherhood. In most traditional patterns of living, a woman's youth and her adult years were fully occupied with the needs of her family. If she survived into old age, then there was normally a place left for her in the home of her children, where her experience and practical help could still be of value.

Such a life cycle, at a time when child-bearing was both more hazardous and inevitable than it is now, might be somewhat relentless but certainly not discontinuous. Where the cohesiveness that comes from an absolute centering on motherhood remains today, it has taken on a different quality. For example, the authors of a study of working-class wives report that this way of looking at one's life cycle is still quite basic to the type of woman they studied: "Before she becomes a wife, and then a mother, she regards herself as getting ready for that role decreed by society and nature; as her children grow up the working class woman is inclined to feel that her life is 'over.' It is in the child-bearing and mothering years, then, that we find the working class woman most fully engaged with life."[1]

This philosophical attitude towards one's life presents no particular problems if life is nearly over, but if thirty or more years of physical life remain, the picture is quite different. A "disengaged" life that persists for several dec-

[1] Lee Rainwater, Richard P. Coleman, Gerald Handel, *Workingman's Wife*, Oceana Publications, Dobbs Ferry, N.Y., 1959, p. 19.

ades is rather alarming, and it is, in *fact*, a discontinuous life, even though most of the conflicting motives that create discontinuity in the life of the educated, middle-class woman are not there. Unresolved conflicts in lifetime motivation are more typical of the educated woman than over-simplification, but her failure to resolve them may lead to a "disengaged" middle age not unlike that of the working-class woman. The fact that various possibilities in life at one time seemed open to her, however, make her preparation for adulthood utterly different. Whatever else it may be, it was quite clearly not a time of "getting ready for that role decreed by society and nature."

Although a woman's "preparation for life" may pull her in several directions at once, the feeblest pull of all is any serious preparation for domesticity and motherhood. Both home and school combine to minimize any practical preparation in most cases, although some home-economics majors and capable "mother's helpers" continue to emerge. The reason for this on the part of the school is fairly self-evident. An intelligent girl in this country is educated like an intelligent boy. She not only takes the same courses—it is tacitly assumed that she is taking them for the same purpose. In this scheme of things, boys are educated to be engineers, businessmen, doctors, or lawyers, but certainly not to be husbands and fathers; and by the same logic, their prospective brides are trained as teachers, nurses, secretaries, or scientists—almost anything but being housewife or mother. If one does not look beyond graduation day, it is all rather logical.

What is somewhat less comprehensible is the attitude of parents towards both the practicalities and probabilities of their daughters' future. There are perfectly good arguments for keeping household training out of higher education, but virtually none for excluding it from the home. Nevertheless, unless a teenage girl is an older sister in a large family, the chances of her getting any real apprenticeship in domesticity are slight. Still less is she encouraged to give any serious thought as to what the nature or pattern of her married life may be. The notion of getting married is held out as very urgent indeed—so important that a precocious sexuality is forced on her long before she is really ready for it, and in a way that seriously conflicts with her educational aims. A sober estimate of what married life may require of her does not accompany this urgency.

The difficulty of combining a prolonged higher education with a premature sex-consciousness is not simply a problem for girls in our society. "Our whole present policy in the upbringing of the young is paradoxical," Arnold Toynbee has heatedly observed. "While we are lowering the age of sexual awareness—and frequently the age of sexual experience, too—to a veritably Hindu degree, we are at the same time prolonging the length of education. We force our boys and girls to become sex-conscious at 12 or 13, and then we ask them to prolong their postgraduate studies till they are nearly 30. . . . If we persist, in this vital matter, on our present Hindu course, our brand new would-be institutions for higher learning will become, in practice, little more than social clubs for sexual mating. This relapse into precocious sexuality," he adds "is one of the moral blemishes of the contemporary Western civilization."[2]

If the problem is not the girl's alone, however, it does

[2] "Why I Dislike Western Civilization," in *The New York Times Magazine*, May 10, 1964.

affect the two sexes in different ways. While Toynbee does not say where the blame for this precocity is to be placed, it is perhaps too often laid at the door of the parents of female offspring, as they are far more apt than the parents of boys to see an early marriage as a satisfactory solution to the problems of growing up. Nor are girls necessarily blocked or hampered in the same way by such marriages from achieving their occupational goals. At least one such goal is apparently achieved, for many girls of college age are, in fact, pursuing not one but two quite contradictory roles at the same time.

It is most improbable that a boy would, for instance, take his professional training as a doctor with the idea that, if he marries, he will quit the medical profession instantly and forever. Nevertheless, this is precisely the mind-set of any number of young women who are taking extensive and expensive vocational training. They may have quite exact and realistic ideas of the steps they need to take in order to arrive at their chosen "occupational identity," and be prepared for the hard work it will take; at the same time, however, they are able to cherish another vision of their occupational future that includes husband, home, and children, but no "outside work" whatever. Where there is an intention to combine the two plans—and one study of college girls showed that about 50 per cent of the girls did intend to combine work and marriage—there is seldom a realistic idea of how the two might be meshed together.[3]

Sidonie Gruenberg, and her daughter Hilda Krech, who studied this conflict in plans rather extensively, are inclined

[3] See Komarovsky, *Women in the Modern World*, pp. 93–94, 97–98.

to lay the blame for confusion on the parents: "By dangling before their daughters two goals (both enticing, both theoretically possible) and by ignoring the fact that the two goals will probably be mutually exclusive, they are in effect putting blinders on their daughters. And these blinders are kept on them all through the period which is primarily devoted to preparing them for life!"[4]

In one sense, the double goal which these parents are dangling is quite necessary. Even if marriage is the primary goal as far as both daughter and parents are concerned, there is no absolute certainty that the goal will be achieved. The ability to support oneself in a more or less interesting manner is a practical way of hedging one's bets. Even if one does "achieve" marriage, this ability is a security against possible financial disasters. What is quite unnecessary, however, and even seriously irresponsible, is the failure to recognize that one is not facing two equally possible alternatives, but the *probability* of marriage. If the young woman faces this probability realistically, she is then confronted with the necessity of making her vocational preparation fit into that probability, however loosely and tentatively. Moreover, even without "blinders," the problems of these years are difficult enough for a young girl. What Toynbee calls our "present Hindu course" has put a social pressure on girls to make an early marriage that is simply not applied to boys. A young woman may have a strong instinct to try to find her own path, her individual way of approaching life, before she enters marriage, but the time to find it is grudged her. (Viz.: Many young men, especially

[4] Gruenberg and Krech, *The Many Lives of Modern Woman*, p. 44.

those in college, are not prepared to marry until they have completed graduate courses and have somewhat established themselves in their vocational work. On the other hand, the woman who has not married by the time she is 25 is regarded as a social failure. It is not until men have reached their mid-thirties that they are subject to this same kind of sympathy.)

There are several aspects of this situation which need to be clearly understood. The first is that a woman's fulfilling herself in her own personal way is quite as necessary for the success of her future marriage as it is for success in creative work of any kind. For woman, but most of all for Christian woman whose marriage is irrevocable, there is no question of making marriage a short-cut to self-realization, or any easy way out of one's dilemmas. Christian marriage in American society provides no escapes, no cosy shelter. It is rather more like an arena. Only a marriage between two mature people who love each other can be fully successful. But the chances of marrying out of genuine love, when one is desperately competing in the "marriage market" in order to find a solution for one's problems, are not very good.

Single-mindedness in the pursuit of one's work may make it possible to avoid certain pitfalls inherent in this stage of life. It certainly makes self-deception in love rather less likely, and it also minimizes the possibility of another kind of deception which competing for a mate is apt to involve, that of "playing dumb" in order to attract popularity. Also, it rules out the yet more dangerous trap of actually stopping dead in one's tracks and arresting one's own development.

There is a reversion, in this whole problem of women deliberately holding themselves back in order to attract men, to the already discussed necessity for "being oneself." In this context, that is, of allowing oneself to develop fully and freely, "being oneself" seems to have overtones of both morality and plain common sense. Intellectual muscle-flexing, or the "I can do anything better than you can" spirit, is certainly not the ideal in relationships between young men and women—it is rather unlovely, if not self-defeating as well. But then, so too is a relationship that was entered into insincerely. It is no rare phenomenon to have a marriage—and one of long standing at that—in which the woman supports the tottering prestige of her husband by throttling any evidence of her own talents. While this alternative may be preferable to the other of letting the marriage fall apart, it cannot be taken as the norm for masculine-feminine relationships, or as a sound basis for entering on a marriage. A shared life of mutual companionship shouldn't mean that the woman has to embark on an intellectual diet. Not only respect for the gifts of God, but common sense as well, suggest that the best way out of this dilemma of self-development for a woman today is to take a positive course. There is absolutely no reason why the pursuit of study and work should disable a young woman for a future lifelong relationship with a man.

This does not mean, however, that the problem of discontinuity in a woman's life would be thereby categorically abolished. In one sense, it makes little difference whether the transition to marriage is made directly from college life, or whether it means dropping out of an already established work life—one sort of world is no preparation for the other. In either case, there will be not only the question of suddenly adjusting to the shared life of intimacy with another person which every marriage, even in the most continuous life cycle involves, but adjustment to the often unfamiliar practicalities involved in housework, cooking, and—usually in short order—small children. Very often, this means a switch from a life that is almost one-sidedly cerebral to a life disconcertingly and uncompromisingly physical. For a buoyant and optimistic young woman, the change may be welcomed as a chance to explore, in the interest of someone she loves, a rather neglected side of her nature. But it is a change, nevertheless, and for some women a rather sharp wrench. In the sense that a well-established rhythm of life is harder to break than one only begun, the woman who is well into some kind of life work may have a harder time.

One study of working women who were attempting this adjustment to domestic life suggests some of the problems. For some of them, there was difficulty in accepting the fact of economic dependency, but even in cases where this was considered no hardship at all, discontinuity meant "the disruption of a whole network of daily habits"[5] and establishing, sometimes painfully, "new rhythms of work" that had no relationship at all to the familiar five-day work-week and the eight-hour working day. It meant, in fact, "a substitution of self-discipline for external controls in planning the day's activities," and a rather lonely discipline at the outset, for leaving her place of work usually meant "a break in group identification" and with it a "loss of self-esteem."[6] To put it bluntly, discontinuity at this stage in life quite often means a shift from easy competence to blundering inefficiency.

[5] Komarovsky, *Women in the Modern World*, p. 138.
[6] *Ibid.*, pp. 140, 142.

The transition at this stage could be, and sometimes is, made smoother by approaching the probability of marriage with a single-minded concentration on homemaking. A woman can accumulate courses in slip-cover-making, home-canning, child psychology, managing the family budget, and hope to enter married life an expert; but single-mindedness of any sort never has quite the effect that was intended when it is applied to anybody's life cycle. In this case, a woman runs the risk of becoming a formidable housekeeper but a dreary companion. The number of conversations between husband and wife that can be spun out on the nutritional content of green and yellow vegetables or how to handle toilet-training is small.

Another possible result which could be at least as serious is that a superficial continuity achieved at this stage in life can only exact a far more painful discontinuity in middle age. There are certainly women for whom domestic interests can successfully occupy a whole lifetime. They may be inventive cooks, effortless housekeepers, or simply fortunate beings who almost invariably have the right approach with children—their own or other people's. In any case, they have enough competence and sufficient interest in some aspect of their daily life as housewives to utilize it in some context outside the family when their children have left home. But the young woman who stifles her real interests and abilities in conscientiously preparing for her "career" as a housewife is not in the same position. She will probably be disenchanted with housekeeping long before middle age, and the bridge to a second life, when she finds herself literally out of work at home, may be hard indeed for her to find.

One-sidedness in either a man or a woman is not ideal, but in the matter of shaping an occupational identity, it is a good deal more disastrous for a woman than a man. One way to see the difference is to examine a little more closely the frequent comparison between a man's professional life and motherhood as a "career." It is a comparison that is superficially attractive because it seems to fit the situation in married life rather well at one particular stage: the first ten or twelve years of a marriage. At this point in their lives, the husband is usually working very hard to establish himself in his career and the wife is equally absorbed in the highly demanding cares of a home and small children. Neither one has much time or energy to spare, but in spite of the strains of this period, there is often the sense that each has a real job to do, and that it is worth the doing.

Each one, it is said, has a career. But do they really? If the husband is really growing in his work, and not just filling time and bringing home a pay check, he is taking on more and more responsibility as he grows in experience—and perhaps in additional training as well. At the end of this ten- or twelve-year period, this growth in responsibility is probably still going on. In any event, he is looking forward to two or three decades, perhaps more, of work at the top of his capacity. His wife, on the contrary, as the children enter school and also become old enough to take over some of the work she has been doing, is already approaching the end of the full-time phase of her motherhood. For the typical American woman who is finished with child-bearing around 26, the picture of her career is changing very rapidly. But even in larger families, where the children are born over a longer period of years, the fact that older children are not only able to take care of themselves, but can share in taking care of younger brothers and sisters, and that money for household help may also be more available, makes for a tapering off in the career pattern. Not only the amount of time spent caring for her family, but the attitude behind that care, should be undergoing a definite and radical shift.

Simply from a practical point of view, it is obvious that a single-minded focusing on motherhood as a full-time career is bound to lead to an impasse for the woman whose children are growing up and leaving her. Not many men find their work being cut back while they are still in their middle thirties and retirement just ahead while they are still in their forties. Among careerists, only professional athletes and entertainers who depend on their glamor are likely to find themselves in a similar position.

It may be painful for her to sense that she is being more or less honorably retired without so much as a gold watch in what feels like the middle of life. But more destructive may be the consequent distortion of the woman's attitude towards her family during the waning phase of her motherhood. Is it psychologically possible for her to make herself "unneeded" by her children, if this also means condemning herself to becoming "unneeded" in an absolute sense because her only job in life is over? The difficulties of this whole process of weaning herself from persons dearly loved are great enough without adding the false note of finality that single-mindedness brings in.

Predictably, many women take some form of evasive action rather than face up to the necessity of a shift in attitude. Instead of accepting the task of making herself unneeded, a woman finds new ways of making herself necessary, or dangerously prolongs old ways. Some of the proliferation of after-school activities for children, requiring a mother as chauffeur and entrepreneur, derive from this urgency to prove oneself essential. Not only would these activities come to a halt if it were not for the faithful mother behind the wheel, but in themselves, these activities put the finishing touches on the products of her career, the well-rounded children who can swim, dance, play a musical instrument or a good game of tennis, ride a horse, and so forth.

Indeed, in addition to affecting family relations, this need of a mother to hang on to a life built around her children is quite likely to produce a severely restricted notion of the area of "outside" or community activities, if not a notion that is warped completely out of shape. Instead of focusing on what really needs to be done, whether in neighborhood, parish, or large community, and on what she is best able to do, she is likely to become totally involved in activities which are still family-centered, though on a somewhat expanded stage. As her children's associations widen beyond the home, she dutifully follows them into P.T.A., scouting, and fund-raising activities for the "child-centered" parish.

All this may make her extraordinarily busy, with an impressive engagement calendar and mounting phone and gasoline bills, but increasingly unsure of what this phase of her "career" means in responsibilities to herself, the world about her, and even to her children for whom she is working so hard. She may, for instance, find it increasingly difficult not only to find the time to talk to her children and help them over some of the rougher stretches of their adolescence, but also to find the degree of emotional separation that makes such a conversation possible. If they are almost extensions of herself, end-products of her work who should be reflecting credit on her industry and capability, it is impossible for her to see, to appreciate, sometimes even to tolerate the persons that they actually are or are trying to become. In the struggle to prolong for herself a stage of life that is really coming to an end, she may not even be able, in some cases, to see the things that she should still be doing for her children.

A typical example of this sort of neglect is the lack of preparation given girls for homemaking. There may be various reasons for the shortage of apprentice housekeepers, not excluding the mother's busy after-school schedule, but one of the simplest is that success with her daughters might mean working her way too quickly and obviously out of a job.[7] The young bride who cannot boil an egg, let alone put together a whole dinner, is no puzzle if she is seen in terms of the exigencies of her mother's "career."

In any case, no matter what the evasions or emotional involvements of this waning phase of her motherhood may be, a certain day will arrive when, as Margaret Mead describes it, a woman "will have to face a breakfast table with only one face across it, her husband's, and she will be alone, quite alone, in a home of their own. She is out of a job; her main justification, the work for which she 'gave up everything,' is gone."[8] On this day, if not before, she may realize that the singlemindedness that pushed her husband steadily

[7] See the comments of David Riesman, Nathan Glazer, and Reuel Denny in *The Lonely Crowd* (Yale University Press, New Haven, 1950, p. 54) on housework as self-justification and escape.
[8] *Male and Female*, p. 250.

ahead in his own work, was sadly misplaced in its application to her life.

For some older women, who feel that their one-sidedness has brought them to a dead-end in life, the effects of discontinuity can be quite shattering. Dr. Esther Harding speaks of the obsessive sense of failure which grips many such women, of depression and insomnia, the lack of meaning. "It is as though she drops into a bottomless pit."[9]

Even when the break in life comes earlier, and is far less overwhelming, the wrench of discontinuity may engender a state of mind very similar to that of adolescence, when a person's whole identity seems once again to be brought into question. If a woman is something more than cook, housekeeper, chauffeur, teacher, and guardian of her children, then what *is* that something more, and how can she build the rest of her life around it? Presumably, under all the onion-like layers of past roles and responsibilities there is some solid core of self, but will it be enough to go on with? Outside clues to the meaning and value of her extra life may not be too helpful. A mother would probably not be much encouraged, for instance, by the notion that, biologically speaking, she really has no business still being around after forty-five, although there are ways and means of patching her up and keeping her going. Nor is the view that she is, if educated and untrained, an economically salvageable but rather troublesome entrant into the labor pool, likely to be any more inspiring.[10] Indeed, it might

[9] *The Way of All Women*, pp. 278–279.

[10] Miss Alice Gore King, executive director of the Alumnae Advisory Center, Inc., of New York City, as quoted by Joseph D. Cooper in *A Woman's Guide to Part-Time Jobs* (Doubleday, Garden City, 1963), p. 91, feels that such women needed much

occur to her that her blurred dissatisfaction is not quite menacing enough to focus the attention of that outside world on her problems. Most middle-aged women are not going to turn to drink or narcotics, make scenes in public or tear apart their children's marriages. They are unlikely to picket employment offices or try suicide. Most of them will not even be blatantly unhappy. They may, in some cases, be nuisances—to family, friends, and sometimes the parish priest—but few of them will be threats. There seems little reason to decide quickly what should be done with them, or, more positively, what they have to offer besides cheap labor and/or eager consumption.

Perhaps the most common reaction to the shock of discontinuity is to retreat from the whole effort of finding a new meaning in life, a rediscovered self, and enter upon a prolonged phase of spectator living. Some of the women who assume that their real work in life is now over may be forced by financial pressure into a paid job, but their attitude towards work is one of minimum involvement. The ideal would be a long, and hopefully enjoyable period of retirement.

A certain slant of light is cast on this premature retirement of the middle-aged woman by a sociological study made of older people a few years ago. The study attempted to focus on "disengagement" or a lessening in active in-

counseling because "(1) They are unprepared; (2) they don't want to use their skills or past experience; (3) they want long and frequent vacations; (4) they are loath to take retraining or beginning jobs; (5) money is usually not the motive and therefore they can afford the luxury of holding out; (6) they have reached a highly successful and respected position in their community and they seek a job commensurate with this position."

volvement with life and with other people among a group of men and women ranging from late middle age to those in their eighties and nineties. "Disengagement" was, incidentally, rather favorably regarded as a realistic approach to the problems of old age by the authors of the survey: "The anticipation of death frees us from the obligation to participate in the ongoing stream of life. If there is only a little time left, there is no point in planning for a future, and no point in putting off today's gratification."[11] This attitude, embodied in a flesh-and-blood "successful-ager," might not strike many viewers as particularly appealing, however. One such example given was Mrs. Clark, a 69-year-old widow: "One reason for Mrs. Clark's general sense of satisfaction is the extent to which she has allowed her own indulgences to grow. When we asked her what things are really less interesting and less enjoyable, she put us in our place by reporting, 'I don't know. I don't *do* anything that I don't want to.' In our terms, Mrs. Clark is a successful-ager because she has completely disengaged from the bonds of earlier relations and has done so in good spirits. . . . she is neither lonely nor disenchanted, pleasing herself by increased small indulgences and not doing 'anything I don't want to.' "[12]

The implication of this study is that "disengagement" takes place rather late in life, as a more or less immediate anticipation of death. But if one looks at the process of aging as these authors describe it, it seems more probable that the real process of disengagement takes place much

[11] Elaine Cumming and William E. Henry, *Growing Old*, Basic Books, New York, 1961, p. 226.
[12] *Ibid.*, pp. 183–184.

earlier in women, and that what is being described is a shift from active to passive spectatorship. For instance, as an example of an "engaged" woman they give Mrs. Brown, mother of eight, who is now 62: "When asked to check a list of various activities that had given her most satisfaction when she was forty-five, Mrs. Brown checks: (1) Just being with your family at home, (2) Keeping house, (3) Church work with fellow church-workers. Now however, she ignores these family-bound activities *and instead checks those reflecting lessened responsibility and 'going'*: (1) Spending time with close friends, (2) Going downtown and shopping around, (3) Going out to eat, (4) Keeping up with the news and what's going on in the world. . . . When asked what things tend to annoy her now, she says, 'Well, one thing, because I'm getting older, the children and the noise. I get to where you can't take it any more like you used to.' The contrast between these statements and her earlier, happier reports of child care and the joys of motherhood is striking."[13]

Some time between 45 and 62, the wrench of discontinuity separated Mrs. Brown from any deep involvement with children, husband, church, or responsible work of any sort. The underlying sense that there is no responsible contribution to be made in this "poorly structured" phase of life is disengagement in the deepest sense. That Mrs. Brown is not untypical of women of her age is suggested by the general contrast made between older men and women: "People who have worked with recreation groups for the aged assure us that old women love to be on the move. They enjoy bus rides and outings, just for the fun of moving

[13] *Ibid.*, pp. 178, 176.

around, while men, in contrast, prefer activities to be useful or educational . . . women in their new freedom, achieve a kind of activity that is a kind of counterpoise to their life experience. Certainly, our empirical observations suggest that the disengaged older man is a thoughtful, reflective, perhaps somewhat opinionated 'wise man,' while the disengaged older woman is an active, carefree, perhaps even frivolous 'girl.' "[14]

Although very old people whom the authors observed, those in their eighties and nineties, showed little sexual difference, both displaying "the same pattern of dependency, self-satisfaction, self-centeredness, and placidity,"[15] the effort to find any real meaning in one's life, either in purposeful activity or deepened reflectiveness, was abandoned much earlier by women than by men. With the cohesiveness that would give their lives a continuing purpose apparently gone, they substituted the "counterpoise" of "going": motion without direction.

In effect, this sort of triviality of life is one response to the discontinuity of middle age. In countless variations and more sophisticated elaborations, sociality, eating out, shopping around, keeping up with the news or gossip—perhaps an unskilled, time-killing job—become the mainstays of an attenuated way of life. Triviality is the pitfall of the one-sided, but it is by no means the only outcome—or pitfall—of discontinuity.

The woman who had strong interests in some sort of non-domestic work before her marriage, who was, perhaps, quite well established in this work, and then abandoned it

[14] *Ibid.*, p. 158.
[15] *Ibid.*, p. 176.

to raise her children, may have a wholly different approach to middle age. She may feel that she can now take up where she left off. Possibly, she sees herself as reëntering a race for status and professional recognition in which she has only temporarily dropped behind. But ordinarily, in spite of the brilliant exceptions, a woman does not find her place again easily after an absence of twenty years. Indeed, if a woman has stayed at home until middle age, she has made a choice that few women who were anxious for advancement were willing to make. The particular skill that she had to offer may have rusted with disuse, or the type of work itself changed radically in the intervening years. Moreover, the particular place that she might have achieved for herself in the business or professional world has apparently been taken by someone else. At a time in life when she may be feeling rather shaky both physically and emotionally,[16] she will probably have to face the effort of retraining, the prejudice of employers against "older women," and the setback of reëntering at a lower level than she had expected. If she sees herself as truly in a race, then the rest of her life may be simply an exhausting struggle to catch up. For an exceptionally talented or determined woman, these handicaps may seem like a challenge, but for the less able, ap-

[16] In noting the possible effects of the menopause on the middle-aged woman's effectiveness in competing in the working world, Maxine Davis remarks that while "only a fifth of all women suffer serious disturbances, and medical science can usually alleviate even the most acute symptoms," the "menopause does constitute bad luck for the woman re-entering her business or profession or starting out for the first time. It may interfere with one's assurance and composure and might increase natural timidity and fears . . ." Getting the Most out of Your Best Years, Dial, New York, 1960, pp. 204–205.

proaching a "second life" in this way must be self-defeating, another dead-end.

In either case, there is a fresh hazard of discontinuity in the whole notion that this stage in a woman's life represents a return to her pre-marital interests. A genuine cohesiveness of life would have to include and build upon the years of marriage, not set them aside as irrelevant. What is at stake, after all, is not simply a continuity or discontinuity of work life, but the relationship between husband and wife. At the time when the children leave home, both of them may be very much tempted to withdraw into a half-remembered pattern of separate existences. One writer, who feels that the "chief peril of this period of life is ambition," suggests that the middle-aged husband and wife risk this attitude of withdrawal into egotism and self-sufficiency: "Let us each take up the threads of our individual lives where we dropped them at the time of our marriage. Let us each in our own way do the things we have always wanted to do in the rush of our everyday affairs."[17] Such an attitude would probably lead few women into a kind of life where they were physically absent from home for months at a time. But however conventional their living pattern, many more absent themselves in spirit from the community of marriage in the conviction that only now, with the entanglements of domestic life behind them, can they pursue their true goals.

Motherhood as a detour in the serious business of life is the most attractive view of her discontinuous life for the educated woman today—and is at least as deceptive as the view of motherhood as a fulltime, lifetime career. As one

[17] Reginald Trevett, *The Tree of Life. Sexuality and the Growth of Personality*, P. J. Kenedy & Sons, New York, 1963, pp. 174–175.

program for women sets it forth, "the hope is that in the course of time there might emerge in the undergraduate a new psychology through which she could look upon the early years of her marriage, the child-bearing period, as only *a temporary and partial interruption to the obligation to use her education* [my italics] extensively and meaningfully rather than as an automatic termination to that obligation— an interruption whose bad effects can be obviated if she will but plan wisely and largely.[18] This is as neat a separation of the meaningless from the meaningful phases of life as any single-minded emphasis on motherhood could possibly provide. The only difference is that the "significant" phases of life have been reversed.

Catholic women may be more inclined than other American women with higher education to view motherhood as a "career" rather than as an "interruption." From a purely practical point of view, the "interruption" is likely to be a longer and more extensive part of the Catholic woman's life than it is for her non-Catholic counterpart.[19] It would be a mistake, however, to accept either view as more correct, or

[18] From the program for the Radcliffe Institute for Independent Study as quoted in Maule, *Executive Careers for Women,* p. 226.

[19] Some statistics suggest that it is particularly the middle-class Catholic woman with a higher education, rather than the less educated, who is likely to have a larger family than her non-Catholic counterpart. Father Thomas in *The American Catholic Family* cites some of the relatively few comparative studies of fertility rates including a rather comprehensive study made in 1941 in Indianapolis: "On the basis of the wife's education, the fertility rate for Catholic couples exceeds that for Protestant couples by 40 per cent at the college level, but by only 3 per cent at the grammar school level." P. 143. More recently, a study by Father Eugene J. Schallert, S. J., of the religious practice of Catholics in Western parishes, also suggests a correlation between higher education and larger families.

even as more appropriate to the circumstances of the Christian woman. A truly Christian view of life simply would not accept either of these easy devaluations of whose stages of her life cycle. As Father LaFarge has asserted, "Life is still a gift, it is an infinitely precious gift as long as you can still speak, or think or say Amen."[20] If this is true of the end of life, it is true of every part of life. A Christian way of approaching the present discontinuities in a married woman's life cycle cannot be to make one stage—any stage—significant, and the rest irrelevant.

Discontinuity, however, is only one of the problems which time poses for the married woman. Before we attempt any solutions or suggestions, therefore, we will go on to another major obstacle, distraction, which so often characterizes a woman's day-to-day life.

[20] *Reflections on Growing Old*, Doubleday, Garden City, 1963, p. 125.

V

The Distracted Life

It is not only possible but quite just to say some very moving and lyrical things about a woman deeply immersed in the activities of motherhood. Gertrud von le Fort, for instance, speaks warmly of the maternal woman who, "overwhelmed as she is by the needs of every day . . . is the great conqueror of the every day. Daily she controls it anew by making it bearable, and her victory is greatest when least observed."[1]

Without denying the truth of this statement, however, we think it a good idea for the Christian housewife and mother, actual or potential, to examine a less flattering view. There is a hint of such a view in Miss von le Fort's word "overwhelmed," but Ignace Lepp has been more explicit: "The usual occupations and preoccupations of a young married woman leave her little time and energy for all the other interests in life. . . . I have known few of my former students—then brilliant, cultivated, and intensely alive mentally and spiritually—who were still capable of rising above the banalities of daily life after ten or twelve

[1] *The Eternal Woman*, Bruce, Milwaukee, 1954, p. 80.

years of married life, or with whom a prolonged conversation could be of any interest."[2] On the basis of his observations as a practicing psychologist, furthermore, Father Lepp states bluntly that it "is relatively rare that married life is not prejudicial to the complete personal development of a woman."[3]

In a sense, the statements by these two authors are not as contradictory as they may seem. The young woman who is the "conqueror of the every day . . . making it bearable" for her family may also be the distressingly dull conversationalist who can't seem to lift herself above the "banalities" of everyday life. That she might be one and the same person is suggested by a further statement of Miss von le Fort's: "The natural and immeasurable love that streams from the mother, and as it were constitutes the shelter within which the child grows to its stature as a person, means for the mother surrender and sacrifice to the point of placing her own stature and her own personality in jeopardy."[4]

Admittedly, there is sometimes a tendency to dramatize the mother's altruism. Helene Deutsch, for example, in attempting to sum up this altruism, says of it "that with regard to the child the mother is completely selfless and willing to sacrifice everything, including her life."[5] But the emphasis in the sacrifice which puts personality in jeopardy is that "it is bound to that which is average and everyday."[6] The clue, then, to the jeopardy or lack of full development

[2] The Psychology of Loving, p. 140.
[3] Ibid., p. 139.
[4] The Eternal Woman, p. 72.
[5] Psychology of Women, volume two, Motherhood, 1945, p. 265.
[6] Von le Fort, The Eternal Woman, p. 73.

of personality, does not lie in extraordinary situations, but in the banality—or heroism—of everyday life. It is right here that we come to face the real problem. We have stressed the fact that the dilemmas and presumably the solutions for the educated laywomen in married life are individual and specific, that it is difficult to speak profitably about "Woman and Daily Life" in the abstract. There is something rather irritating, in fact, about any bland elimination of differences, no matter how well meaning. When a perceptive writer such as Phyllis McGinley says of housewives, "We may be merely directing servants and altering flower arrangements. Or we may be weaving the very wool which goes into the family blankets. It is all one . . . ,"[7] the inclination is to reject this statement rather testily. It may be "all one" from the point of view of the housewife's ultimate responsibility, but it is not all one in the effect on mind and spirit of the housewife and mother whether she is totally engaged in manual labor or relatively free to balance her daily life in other directions.

The mother of two and the mother of ten do not normally have quite the same problems. In fact, the mother of ten—or seven, or twelve—may reject with justifiable derision the notion that her problem is over-concentration on the individual child or a too zealous attention to the finishing touches of ballet dancing or horseback riding. The difficulties of the woman raising her children in the protected, "homogenized" world of the suburbs are not those of a city woman in a deteriorating neighborhood; nor, as we have already seen, is the housewife's daily life at all what it would

[7] *Sixpence in Her Shoe*, Macmillan, New York, 1964, pp. 7–8.

have been seventy, forty, or even less than twenty years ago in this country.

Is there a sense, then, in which one can talk about the daily lives of housewives and mothers as if there were some truly relevant common denominator—a shared problem of dailyness that is experienced to a significant degree by all of them? If one concentrates on a particular phase of life, the early stage of marriage when there are several small children at home all day, the answer is, probably, yes.

There are different names for this common denominator. Chesterton praised it as "universality." Jacques Barzun characterizes it more bluntly as "interruption,"[8] and Anne Morrow Lindbergh produces the formidable German word "Zerrissenheit," or "torn-to-pieces-hood." But the simpler name of "distraction," which she gives to this common denominator in another passage, seems as good a word as any. "I begin to understand why the saints were rarely married women," she writes. "I am convinced it has nothing inherently to do, as I once supposed, with chastity or children. It has to do primarily with distractions. The bearing, rearing, feeding and educating of children; the running of a house with its thousand details; human relationships with their myriad pulls—woman's normal occupations in general run counter to creative life, or contemplative life, or saintly life."[9]

One may take a more optimistic view than Mrs. Lindbergh does of the practising housewife's prospects of sanctity, and still see that she has touched on a problem which

---

[8] "Whereas the very essence of thought is continuity, the very essence of domestic life is interruption." *Teacher in America,* Atlantic-Little, Brown, Boston, 1945, p. 243.

[9] *Gift from the Sea,* Pantheon, New York, 1955, p. 29.

accounts for much of the lack of development which we
have been examining. What is sketched in with all these
remarks is a picture that is familiar and "traditional," and at
the same time puzzlingly new. The multiple claims on a
housewife and mother's time and energy, briefly described
here, are altogether familiar. Even the Valiant Woman in
Proverbs was described as having "risen in the night" so that
she might have enough time to get through her daily round.
What is it, then, that makes "distraction" a new dilemma
for married women?

There is no one simple answer. All the factors of change
discussed in our first chapter enter in and more besides.
But there are three possible lines of explanation, not mutually exclusive, but ordinarily reinforcing each other. One
of them lies in the physical milieu of contemporary housekeeping; another in the conflicting demands that are being
made on marriage and motherhood today; and the third in
the changed expectations of the woman herself.

Once again, as in the question of discontinuity, and for
much the same reasons, the conflicts and expectations are
mainly those of the educated, middle-class woman. This is
not to say that the working-class wife necessarily finds housekeeping much more satisfactory. The first reason—the
change in physical conditions—certainly affects the working-class wife equally and perhaps even more. Her education has given her fewer inner resources to combat the
loneliness and isolation which is the characteristic difficulty
of this new milieu; and it is, in fact, loneliness, quite as
much as financial pressures, that sometimes drives married
women in this class into otherwise unglamorous industrial
and service jobs.

Not only is the isolation of the housewife a factor that cuts across classes, but the change in the kind of work done necessarily affects all women. By and large, while these changes have made housework physically less strenuous, they have also managed to make it less satisfying by removing from it the element of creativity. More than this, the sort of "distraction" that comes from trying to do two or more physically contradictory things at the same time—for instance, get dinner ready and keep one's eye on several small children, who may need more or less simultaneously to be fed, changed, and otherwise diverted—seems to be quite universal. Only a thoroughly phlegmatic temperament, or perhaps heroic sanctity, can mitigate it.

But the special quality of distraction that comes from more profoundly conflicting demands bears harder on the educated than the working-class woman. There is not, for instance, the same sort of conflict between preoccupation with child-raising and companionship with one's husband, not because the practical difficulties are very different, but because many working-class husbands express no desire for such companionship. The situation described in the Rainwater-Lee-Coleman sociological study of working-class wives may not be particularly satisfactory, but it is not one of distraction between apparently conflicting goals: "When we look at the ways in which husbands and wives interact in the working class, we find a pattern of relative isolation, and a tendency for their roles to be rather sharply demarcated. . . . The couple's day seems to be spent in isolated activity, with a minimum amount of time spent around shared interests. There seems to be a greater division of labor and interest between husband and wife in the working class than in the middle class. Often we find the wife a little unhappy about her isolation, but feeling that this is the way her husband prefers it."[10] Unquestionably, this sort of life is a great deal less than what educated couples, looking for a complete personal union, a genuine sharing of life and love, would be willing to settle for. Although this particular sort of dreariness may not lie ahead of them, they may nevertheless find themselves sharing a great deal less than they had hoped, and, paradoxically, sharing a little less with every passing year.

Young people who marry today have even more reason than their parents—and their grandparents—to hope that they will be each other's life-long friend as well as lover and partner in a common enterprise. The mobility, the shifting about from job to job, neighborhood to neighborhood, one region of the country to another, uproots family ties and lasting friendships. The constant, the dependable element in all this change should be the companionship of husband and wife, for if the marriage has begun with genuine friendship as well as love, with a real interweaving of interests, the expectation is that this is something which will solidify and grow with each passing year.

Too often, in spite of both expectation and necessity, this is not what happens. Rather, what is happening in too many cases is the erosion not the building-up of intimacy, an erosion that may remain well concealed for years under the façade of the business—and busyness—of family life. When the façade finally collapses, the marriage itself, as a living relationship, may tumble with it.

This is certainly a problem that is being taken more and

[10] Workingman's Wife, p. 76.

more seriously in relation to Christian marriage, but unless
it is clearly grasped in its prosaic context of day-by-day
"distraction," its real nature and possible solution will remain elusive. For what is being eroded in the course of
daily life might be being built up, or at the least maintained,
if only the conflicting demands of the every day were better
understood.

Obviously, the first person who needs to understand the
nature of these demands is the married woman herself. If
she sees the situation as having "a duty towards everybody
but herself"—to use Barzun's apt description, so that "her
mind necessarily reverts to the feral state,"[11] she is most
certainly not viewing it all very clearly. This is maternal
altruism run amok. Too often, it seems that the first com-
modity to disappear during the years of early motherhood is
the sense of proportion. There is a transformation, sometimes rather sudden, from a person who disposes of her
time and energy to a person disposed of, passing from one
demand upon her to another—she has as little control and
conscious direction as a twig in a tornado.

More than likely, this transformation is begun when the
new mother is suddenly faced with the "crisis" situation of
being totally responsible for a small and utterly dependent
human being. If taking care of a new baby is completely unfamiliar to her, the atmosphere of extreme pressure in which
one's sense of proportion can easily vanish can be overwhelming. Even if the young wife has been through all the
motions of bathing, feeding, changing, and soothing small
babies before, her feeling that her particular baby's life, in
so many ways, depends altogether on her care, may quite
override any other considerations.

[11] *Teacher in America*, p. 243.

Next to the baby, the husband of such a woman is apt
to look monstrously self-sufficient. Though he may not like
the idea, he is quite capable of getting his own breakfast—
while the baby would starve without the mother's atten-
tions. If she takes her eye off her husband for a moment, he
is hardly likely in the meantime to roll off the bed and hit
his head, or drown in a bathtub. Furthermore, he is altogether free, compared not only to the baby but suddenly
to the baby's mother as well, to go wherever he pleases. The
young mother comes to realize that this dependency of her
child on her is as well a leash on her own freedom of movement.

With the coming of children, there is a real shift from
one emphasis in the daily life of marriage to another. Erikson has called it the change from intimacy to generativity.
As he points out, the "strength acquired at any stage [in
life] is tested by the necessity to transcend it in such a way
that the individual can take chances with what was most
vulnerably precious in the previous one."[12] There is no real
gain in maturity, if one or both of the partners in a marriage
try to retain the *status* quo of intimacy at the cost of evad-
ing the burdens—and joys—of generativity. Nevertheless,
intimacy, the vulnerable companionship built up in the
early period of courtship and marriage, is only supposed to
lessen, not disappear. The chances that are being taken with
it, quite necessarily, have to be seen in order to be mini-
mized, and it is just the capacity for this clear-eyed view that
is likely to disappear with "distractions."

One of the most obvious chances taken is with the relationship of husband and wife as lovers, but even if the
decline at this level of intimacy is at least as disappointing

[12] *Childhood and Society*, p. 263.

as the change in conversation, it may not be at all plain what is going wrong. The whole area of sexual adjustment is one where harmony may be rather delicate and precarious under the best of circumstances. Although it is as perilous to generalize about male and female sexuality as it is about any other characteristic, there seems to be a rather common problem of adjusting two markedly different needs or drives. Ernest Havemann has observed in this connection: "The forgotten lesson of the Kinsey report is simply this: The average man's sexual appetite starts earlier, is stronger, and lasts longer than anybody but a thoroughly candid and uninhibited male realizes. But the average woman's sexual appetite starts late and is far weaker than anybody but a thoroughly candid and unpretentious woman would dare to admit. . . . The important fact about . . . the average woman . . . is that she can take sex or leave it alone. . . . She is far more likely to regard it as a mere pleasant happenstance, an unimportant side issue, or even a nuisance than as the goal of life."[13]

The years of early motherhood, when the greatest demands are made on a woman's day-to-day reserve of energy, are more likely to provide the worst than the best circumstances for sexual adjustment. If, as one study of female sexuality has shown, "the two major deterrents to basic female sexual responsiveness are fatigue and preoccupation,"[14] both deterrents are likely to be in abundant supply during the years when there are babies and small children in the home. What is perhaps most difficult for the husband to accept is that, in the midst of a host of seemingly

[13] *Men, Women & Marriage*, Monarch Books, 1963, p. 30–31.
[14] Quoted in Erikson, *Childhood and Society*, p. 46.

imperative daily demands, stacks of ironing, dishes in the sink, a baby to be fed, and small children to be bathed and put to bed, *his* requests seem to have no special priority. At the end of a hard day, his wife may not be able fully to appreciate that sexual intercourse is the act which should be the total expression of their love, and not just one last chore for the day. And even though this fuzziness of vision about one central area of married life is only an obvious, not an isolated instance of the effects of distraction, it is a critical one.

Perhaps we should not blame only "fatigue and pre-occupation" in this matter of adjustment. It is certainly coming to be increasingly recognized that for Catholic couples, the problems of achieving a satisfactory sexual re-lationship can be enormously complicated, either by the use of rhythm, more prolonged continence, or simply by the fear of another pregnancy. Whatever the reasons for maladjustment, sexual union is such a basic expression of the self-donation of marriage, though not the only one, that failure in this area is most likely to drive a wedge between a couple. Lack of response at this level of intimacy may only sum up a whole series of strains and imbalances in the relationships of wife, husband, and children, but it is at a level which is singularly difficult to ignore or overlook. It may, in fact, sharply point up the unresolved conflicts im-plied in a changing concept of marriage which requires newly exacting relationships to *both* husband and children, without providing any clear guide lines as to how they should be combined.

The cross-currents and cross-purposes of "distraction" are numerous. The difficulty of maintaining a warm, responsive, and intelligent companionship with one's husband without losing a grip on baby-tending, cleaning, cooking, and chauffeuring is only one of them. But it does epitomize the characteristic effect of distraction, that the married woman, caught in its grip, seems both to herself and to others to be something less of a person than she once was, and more a collection of functions and duties.

However little aware women may be of the long-term effects of distraction, they are often troubled by this sense of diminished personality. Moreover, they connect this loss quite definitely with the multiple demands of their daily life. One study of chronically fatigued patients showed that, "In industry, the most fatiguing jobs are those which only partially occupy the worker's attention, but at the same time prevent him from concentrating on anything else. Many young wives say that this mental gray-out is what bothers them most in caring for home and children. 'After a while your mind becomes a blank,' they say. 'You can't concentrate on anything. It's like sleep-walking.' "[15] One comes upon this same theme repeatedly, wherever the attitude of educated married women towards their life as housewives and mothers is discussed. What seems to be troubling them most is the non-stop quality of their lives, the sense of being perpetually on call. The "mental gray-out" reflects not so much the inevitable outcome of a certain type of work, as it does the absence of any counteracting force in their lives that would make for concentration as against dispersion. What is apparently particularly disturb-

[15] Findings of Baruch Study on Chronic Fatigue Patients as reported in "Why Young Mothers Are Always Tired," *Redbook*, September, 1959.

ing is the lack of any unbroken stretches of time in which the housewife can read, reflect, or do any sort of concentrated work—or simply rest up and refresh herself. Equally troubling is the fact that this hopping from task to task prevents her from specializing in any aspect of her work and really gaining competence in it.

This general dissatisfaction of the housewife, moreover, does not necessarily spring from a contempt for manual work or a dislike of small children. Most likely, a housewife finds most of her work tolerable, and a fair amount of it thoroughly enjoyable. She may take great pleasure in bathing her baby, devising dresses for her small girls, trying out recipes, or reducing a chaotic closet to a momentary state of order. If she is realistic, she assumes that any kind of work has its boring and unpleasant stretches—but few educated married women have actually envisioned spending nearly all their time in drudgery. It is the sum total of days, weeks, months, years of these activities—through which a woman may begin to move more and more somnambulistically—rather than the component parts, which can become so discouraging.

This brief sketch of the "distracted life" may not be gloomy enough to satisfy those who think that the years of early motherhood, taken at full strength with no substitute mothers to alleviate the press of duty, are really utterly dreadful. "Distraction" seems a singularly anemic word for the housewife and mother's predicament when one considers the following passage from The Feminine Mystique: "During the 1950's, psychiatrists, analysts, and doctors in all fields noted that the housewife's syndrome seemed to become increasingly pathological. The mild undiagnosable symptoms—bleeding blisters, malaise, nervousness, and fatique of young housewives—become heart attacks, bleeding ulcers, hypertension, bronchopneumonia; the nameless emotional distress became a psychotic breakdown. Among the new housewife-mothers, in certain sunlit suburbs, this single decade saw a fantastic increase in 'maternal psychoses,' mild-to-suicidal depressions or hallucinations over childbirth."[16]

On the other hand, "distraction" scarcely reinforces the picture of the poised and competent Christian mother one reads about, who turns out Advent wreaths and batches of whole-wheat bread, or leads an attractive and malleable group of children—ages three to fourteen—through an antiphonal recitation of the psalms.

A concentration on distraction certainly does not do justice to what is best in these years. Even the most confused day may have its islands of real joy, and it is highly questionable whether even strongly dissatisfied mothers would want to make a really drastic change in their lives, write these years off, and do without the home and children that they do not know quite *what* to do with. Many more would question the whole assumption that they are dissatisfied—apart from rather minor complaints and regrets—much less that they are on the verge of bleeding ulcers and breakdowns.[17]

[16] P. 293.

[17] George Gallup and Evan Hill in an article on "The American Woman" (*The Saturday Evening Post*, December, 1962) reported the results of a survey of 2,300 women, both married and single which stressed the contentment of married women. 57 per cent of married women as opposed to 29 per cent of the single women reported themselves extremely happy, 39 per cent fairly happy, with 64 per cent of single women in that category; and only 4 per cent

But the point at issue is not really happiness or unhappiness at all, particularly if one is concentrating on one stage of life without any relation to the others; nor is it a calling into question of the values deeply imbedded in these years—any more than it is an attempt to slur over the really desperate problems that some women face in the central period of motherhood. What is brought to a focus in the problem of distraction is the question of development, and, more precisely, of the choices, made consciously or by default, that lead to a certain sort of development. It is one of the peculiarities of the "distracted life" that, by keeping the married woman's attention moored to the demanding and sometimes delightful present, it makes the necessity of specific choices and the whole issue of personal development seem rather insubstantial and irrelevant. Discontinuity becomes unnecessarily sharp because the steps leading up to it are so stealthy. The only jarring note in Dr. George Gallup's survey of happily married American women was the discovery of their rather complacent fixation on the present. The American woman, he says, "has made her choice—not business or politics, but marriage. This single-mindedness probably will bring her trouble. Today, after her youngest child has turned 21, the average American woman has nearly another 30 years of life, and these can be the empty years. . . . Only 31 per cent report that they are 'taking courses or following a plan to improve them-

---

admitted to being not so happy. They were slightly less euphoric on the subject of their achievements, 25 per cent of the married women reporting themselves extremely satisfied, 63 per cent fairly satisfied, and 12 per cent not so satisfied. "Practically every one of the 1813 married women in this survey said that the chief purpose of her life was to be either a good mother or a good wife." Pp. 27–28.

selves,' and almost a third of these involve improving their physical shape or appearance."[18]

But the "choice" of marriage has not eliminated a whole series of choices, however imperceptible they may seem to the woman caught in the daily flow of distraction, and some of the consequences of these choices will fall due long before the youngest child reaches 21. There is, for example, the uncomfortable possibility that everyone in the family will "grow up" with the exception of mother. The dilemmas caused by husbands who move ahead in business or profession and outstrip their wives is a rather familiar one, but this sort of uneven development can take place in relation to the children as well.

There is no safe dividing-line between "selfish" personal development and "maternal altruism," for in the last analysis, the demands of both husband and children cannot be satisfied by supplying hot meals, scrubbed floors, ironed shirts, and safe transportation, if the supplier has turned into a kind of vending machine. The man who ten years ago married a young woman "intensely alive mentally and spiritually," would presumably like to find her again behind the frown of the mother of his children, whose conversational range seems limited to how the children are adjusting to school, or whether the family needs a new car more than it does a new automatic washer.

Our brief discussion of the erosions of distraction is certainly not intended to be a blanket indictment of all married women. Not all intelligent and educated wives, after a few years of exposure to married life, are measured by the dimension of banality, or are boring their husbands and chil-

[18] *Ibid.*, p. 32.

dren to death. A good many wives still have their vitality and their wits about them. Our point is simply that those who are still "intensely alive," even if not *au courant* on every subject from existentialism to Op art, are either blessed with an almost indestructible surplus of energy, or have been more or less purposefully swimming against the tide. The last job to be done, the one that can always be postponed, is that vaguest of all duties, the duty to oneself. All that has been said about women acquiring a greater sense of themselves as persons, of seeing their role in marriage as "uniquely creative," of wanting a more developed and satisfying relationship with their husbands, is quite true as far as it goes. The problem is that, under actual conditions of "distracted" wifelihood, these aspirations, if they were hopes rather than plans, may turn into no more than vague if pricking discontent. The intellectual life is given over to the last blurred minutes before sleep.

The success of Betty Friedan's *The Feminine Mystique*, with its "life-plan" for women, presumably rests on women's growing realization that drifting along in marriage can lead to some unexpected and painful results. It would be unfortunate, however, were this new instinct for purpose and a fuller use of the whole span of life, to be pegged to two children and a professional career. The woman with a large family who prefers to find her "occupational identity" in working for love rather than for money or status, still needs, if only for the sake of her family, the fullest use of her gifts within the framework she has chosen. Both in the long run and in the shorter view of things, this means more planning, more conscious choice between different alternatives, more thought given to education, to leisure, to the activities which extend beyond her home into the community and the world; and more thought to the "second life" in middle age that most probably awaits her.

Perhaps first of all, however, it means a deliberate re-thinking of what the concept of vocation means in relation to her particular life, her whole life.

VI

Vocation

The housewife of today is being urged to pull herself together and tie up the strands. Nor are these admonitions of
the sort that might have come her way in the past: gentle
reminders to separate the light wash from the dark, plan
the week's menu aforehand with a careful scheme for dis-
posing of the leftover roast, or set aside Tuesdays for ironing. Anxiety over the leftover roast as an example of
woman's improvidence has been transferred to such larger
matters as ten-thousand-dollar educations put to no use, or
thirty years of life expended on bridge and begonias. Short-
ages of teachers, nurses, and social workers, typically feminine professions, have occasioned much more critical looks
at woman's wasted training, and have even prompted half-
serious proposals that women be drafted.[1] The Gallop Poll
report on American women suddenly strikes a sour note:
"American society will hardly accept millions of ladies of
leisure—or female drones—in their 40's." The authors report that "Some steps are being taken to thwart this trend
before it becomes a national problem," but they conclude

[1] Marion K. Sanders, "A Proposition for Women," in Harper's
Magazine, September, 1960, is one example.

somewhat crisply that the "American woman is going to have to face this problem herself."[2]

It is in this context of pressure for more planning in women's lives—coming to some extent from public opinion as well as from inner discontent—that the notion of a "life plan" for women, "a lifetime commitment . . . to a field of thought, to work of serious importance to society,"[3] has to be evaluated. For the Christian married woman who may have been prodded into examining her life more sharply, there is another aspect to be considered. At the same time she is being urged to organize a "life plan" and get the next thirty or forty years under tighter control, she is being assured that as a housewife and mother she already has a vocation. What connection, if any, is there between a life plan and a vocation?

If she is given to snap judgments, she might decide that the two terms are mutually exclusive. A life plan, based on the individual woman's "needs and abilities,"[4] is for the housewife who doesn't want to be a housewife; a vocation is for the housewife who *does*. Certainly, the sort of thinking that presents lay vocations for men in sweepingly diverse terms—doctors, lawyers, scientists, policemen, plumbers—and the married woman's vocation quite simply as housewife, encourages this conclusion. But a closer look at the whole idea of lay vocations suggests that while there is a difference between life plan and vocation, it is surely not that one is for the individual and the other is not.

[2] George Gallup and Evan Hill, "The American Woman," p. 32.
[3] Betty Friedan, *The Feminine Mystique*, p. 366.
[4] *Ibid.*, p. 338.

Unfortunately, probing into lay vocations means treading on some rather marshy theological ground. Even such an apparently rudimentary question as the distinction between a lay and a religious vocation, and how one arrives at being a layman or laywoman can open up some singularly baffling problems. For that matter, just what *is* the lay state to which the married woman has presumably been called?

John Gerken, in a complex but forthright study, points out that "the perfection of the lay state insofar as it is *lay* is constituted by marriage, ownership, and adult self-determination,"[5] whereas the "perfection of the religious state is the direct opposite of this . . . the state of the vows of poverty, chastity, and obedience."[6] But the mere fact that one is married, lives in a mortgaged home, and makes decisions on what to have for dinner or where to go on vacation, with no reference to superiors, does not make one a layman.

The layman is a "mature adult Christian," and even more specifically a person committed to a type of action which is distinct from the action of a religious: "The layman is to make the earth habitable, to work for the prosperity of the community, to develop creation in accord with its laws, to struggle for the total dominion of Christ over things, to struggle for the completion of God's plan. . . ."[7] This seems plain enough as far as it goes. The difficulty comes when one *does* proceed a step or two further and tries to explain why one chooses to be a lay person rather than a religious,

[5] *Toward a Theology of the Layman*, Herder and Herder, New York, 1963, p. 10.
[6] *Ibid.*, p. 10.
[7] *Ibid.*, p. 102, 101.

or, to take a related question, why and how the "better state" of consecrated virginity really is superior. A candid attempt to grapple with these questions can be quite disconcerting, for the traditional explanation of the choice, that the lay person, unlike the religious, has chosen to love God with a divided heart, is not altogether satisfactory.

One might take, for instance, this description of the "dividedness" of the married person from a recent book on the theology of marriage: "Being male or female involves something more than the ability to have children. It is part of the most basic feature of a human being, an ability to make a gift of oneself.... When such a gift is made to God, it is psychologically possible to center life on Him as never before. When it is made to a human being, even the most lovable and deserving human being, it cannot be made as readily to God. There is something exclusive about it. The person who tries to make it twice feels himself divided. God can certainly be loved but not with the same spontaneous energy and absorption."[8] Without attempting for the moment to decide whether this description is psychologically apt for the *committed* lay person, one might as well face squarely just what it is that this gift of oneself to another in marriage is supposed to imply, and why it is so critical: "... there is a definite tendency to minimize the importance of a decision to take on a way of life that divides the heart. The layman may be told that, in spite of the fact that virginity and the religious state are better, still his role in the Church is an important one, entailing responsibilities and offering the opportunity for great holiness. In this

[8] Joseph E. Kerns, S.J., *The Theology of Marriage*, Sheed and Ward, New York, 1964, p. 155.

manner of encouragement both the inferiority of the lay
state and the deliberate choice of that inferior state are
glossed over. But it is precisely this decision that has to be
explained. This decision establishes the state of the layman.
If his state is inferior, there must be something inferior
about his decision. If there is something inferior about his
decision, then there must be something about it inimical
to the kingdom of God."[9]

Despite the clerical tone of Father Gerken's remarks—
and disregarding for the moment the very debatable sup-
position that virginity and the religious state are "better"—
it will seem to many lay people that Father Gerken has over-
estimated the importance of the actual *decision*. This is a
crucial point. It is perfectly natural for a religious, who has
undergone a long novitiate and period of testing, to see the
decision itself to enter a particular state of life as critical.
One does not wake up suddenly to find oneself a religious.
Even so, it is in a sense quite frequent that "suddenly" a
man and woman find themselves married—and the woman
especially. Not infrequently, and always irrevocably, a man
and woman enter into marriage without either genuine
maturity or the necessary information and guidance which
would make a clear-cut choice between the two ways of life
possible. An obvious example is the non-Catholic "taking
instructions" who has married before her conversion: there
is simply no question of her having made a decision between
the two states, second-rate or otherwise. There are also less
glaring instances—early marriage, lack of an adequate religious education—which cast some doubt on the crucial
importance of the decision to enter a particular state of life.

[9] Gerken, *Toward a Theology of the Layman*, p. 14.

In many such cases, the person may become a mature, adult, committed Christian, and so a layman in the full sense, years after that decision has been technically made.

Nevertheless, the whole question about the nature of that state, once entered, is singularly troublesome. To say that the lay person loves God with a divided heart is to say that he or she loves God with a lukewarm and leftover love, and that the source of this lukewarmness is the love for one's partner in Christian marriage. This stance is thoroughly inappropriate towards the growing body of religiously concerned lay people. If one is trying to get at what constitutes the perfection of each state, there seems to be little point in comparing devout religious with mediocre lay people.

There is, however, a still more fundamental flaw in comparing the lay and religious way of loving God as divided, or as indirect and direct, and this flaw lies at the very heart of the problem of the Christian married woman. Unless she has a fundamentally sound sense of her vocation, of what is God's will for her, and what her response to His love should be in the specific circumstances of her married life, she is paralyzed. A "life plan," after all, only makes sense if one has some idea of a purpose in one's life, and the theory of the divided heart leaves her forever at cross purposes. If, when she is devoting herself lovingly to the life of her family, she is, in effect, nudging out the capacity for a love of God, what is she to do?

The fact is that most devout and intelligent married lay-women do not explicitly ask this question, and therefore cannot see their situation in so discouraging a light. In the first place, a woman does not feel, in making a gift of herself to another human being, that she is somehow withdrawing the gift of herself to God—or that the place which God holds in her life detracts from the love of her husband. More than this, her love for her husband, far from being an obstacle, should be a means to a greater love of God.

Of course, this does not mean that love of husband—or family—may not, under certain circumstances, be opposed to the love of God, only that it need not be. Nor does it mean that an awareness of God's presence may not be lost sight of in the midst of day-to-day distractions, and particularly in the absence of any conscious attempt at prayer. It does mean, however, that an intense and loving response to God's love by a married woman can and should be through and not in spite of the circumstances of marriage. Those realities which characterize the lay state, marriage, ownership, and adult self-determination, are the realities upon which *her* holiness must be built. It will not do her the slightest good, for example, to think of herself as a substitute religious, as some kind of married virgin. On the contrary, she must grow in charity, by trying to use her capacity for sexual relationship in a self-giving to her husband that is as loving, considerate of his needs, and generous as she knows how to make it. Her problem is not one of finding other ways to give herself to Christ, but of encompassing the gift to husband and the gift to Christ in one single offering, and of making the sometimes too opaque relationships within her family transparent to the presence of Christ within them.

But if one assumes that both states of life are direct ways of loving God, the question still remains: Why is virginity necessarily the "better way"? This is certainly not the question that can be answered by a married laywoman, who, apart from theological inexperience, would have the practical handicap of a different view of life. According to Gerken, "the betterness of virginity can be said to consist in its ability to manifest the supernatural characteristics of Christian love. Lay life as such cannot manifest this characteristic."[10] Presumably, the inability of family life to manifest the supernatural means, in this context, its inability to manifest the supernatural to others—that is, that the family does not bear witness to another world as religious life does. But one could also point out that this inability, so to speak, can exist within the family circle as well. Very possibly, the growth of interest in family sacramentals, from Advent wreaths to special feast-day dishes, represents a need for the parents to remind themselves of the invisible realities of their situation, quite as much as a means to the Christian education of their children. Family life has few built-in reminders of the supernatural. To say that it can be a direct way of loving God does not mean that it is an easy way.

There are differences in temperament, in the whole cast of mind and heart, that make one's state in life more or less "direct" for each person. Where one woman might find the spring of love seemingly drying up within the structure of religious life, another will find that the less obviously supernatural milieu of family life means for her a disheartening but nonetheless steady growth in materialism. Quite apart from these individual differences, however, it is still necessary to state categorically that marriage is *not*, objectively speaking, the same thing as a vocation to contemplative life. If this may seem too obvious even to men-

[10] *Ibid.*, pp. 90–91.

tion, we are reminded that, on the other hand, there is often nothing so imperceptible as what is the obvious. The seeming formlessness of married life, the vast and legitimate variety of life styles that are embraced in marriage, and, not least, the sense that there is a great deal of useful energy going to waste, all tempt the speculative mind to find a new key to the whole affair. Thus one housewife and mother has surmised that the housewife's present dilemma of isolated manual work is really meant to prod her towards her true vocation of contemplation: "This silence and solitude, aiding and abetting the mysterious interaction of manual labor and study on the soul, is supposed to produce the highest prayer . . . washing children's faces and cooking meals are elements, not of an active life, but of a contemplative life. Housewives are contemplatives."[11]

Not only are all housewives meant to be contemplatives, but they would be making a serious mistake if they attempted to stray in any other direction: "The married woman . . . is a cloistered woman. . . . No matter how active she may be in her proper sphere, the wife and mother's life is fundamentally an enclosed one of prayer, service, and suffering. The spirituality that most approximates hers today might be that of a Dominican, or Carmelite friar, or a Benedictine monk, who may indeed have much contact with the world, but whose methods remain primarily contemplative, and who always keeps at least one foot in the cloister, where the mode of life is both secluded and cenobitic. From what I see about me, married women who see themselves in any other terms wind up crucified in all

[11] Solange Hertz, *Women, Words and Wisdom*, Newman, Westminster, 1959, pp. 79, 81.

directions, spiritually more out of the home than in it. If they are fervent, they become easily embroiled in techniques proper to their husbands or other 'activities' for spreading the Kingdom, and may end by running homes which are little more then madhouses of indoctrination."[12]

The attractiveness of this kind of theorizing is that it strongly emphasizes the importance of prayer in the housewife's life. Mrs. Hertz's idea is thoroughly refreshing in contrast to the spate of literature which assumes, on the other hand, that the housewife can get by comfortably with a morning offering, a few ejaculations throughout the day, and the family rosary at night. But her all-embracing notion of housewives as contemplatives also raises some very serious, and insurmountable, difficulties.

One, as Mrs. Hertz herself acknowledges, is that it is not really all-embracing. "Not every woman is called to live a prayer life in her own home approaching that of the desert fathers," she observes, and few would disagree. Even in religious life, the greatest number of women enter active rather than strictly contemplative orders. But a second difficulty, which is at least as fundamental, is that for those women who feel strongly attracted to a contemplative life, the "distracted" life of a housewife is certainly no royal road to contemplation. The similarity between the "silence and solitude" of the life of a housewife with small children and that of a Benedictine cloister is not usually very striking. Even when the housewife is shelling peas or scrubbing floors, thus freeing her mind for a contemplative flight, no doubt in less than 90 seconds the phone will ring, or the children will begin yelling, or she will suddenly

[12] Hertz, *Searcher of Majesty*, pp. 214–215.

remember that vital ingredient she forgot to buy at the grocery store. At this point, the fact that "intellectual and manual tasks have deep mystical inter-relationships"[13] is likely to escape her. The life of the Carmelite nun or the Benedictine monk, while it would certainly include the pea-shelling and the floor-scrubbing, or its equivalent, is not only comparatively orderly, and silent, but it is ordered around a life of prayer. The housewife's is not. However much she may need and want prayer, her life is ordered around the intersecting and continuous demands of husband, children, pets, and a furnished home that she is obliged to keep habitable in spite of all their efforts to the contrary. She may at times have a deep feeling of sympathy with Thoreau's remark—"I had three pieces of limestone on my desk, but I was terrified to find that they required to be dusted daily, when the furniture of my mind was all un-dusted still, and I threw them out of the window in disgust. How, then, could I have a furnished house?"[14]—but nevertheless, in her laywoman's state of marriage, property, and adult self-determination, she is faced with a furnished apartment, and there are no lease-clauses about throwing things out the window. Instead, she is obliged to dust, sweep, scrub, or hide them.

All this does not mean that the housewife cannot or should not pray, or that she could not make better use of what silence and solitude she does have than turning on the radio. It just means that a woman who feels her vocation is to find Christ in silent contemplation, is picking a very

[13] *Ibid.*, p. 93.
[14] *Walden*, Modern Library edition, Random House, New York, 1937, p. 32.

bumpy and devious road to this goal in housewifery; or, to put it another way, if Christian homes are, by their very nature, cloisters, why have any other kind of cloisters at all?

It is equally doubtful that the housewife's daily life provides a natural springboard for apostolic activity. One may have quite grave doubts that the married woman is meant to be a "cloistered" woman, and still see that she does not have the freedom of operation of a single person. The young woman who has a great desire for direct apostolic action has to take into sober consideration, the fact that it may be only after many years of married life that she will have the time and opportunity to make more than a very negligible contribution. She may be perfectly well aware that as the mother of small children, she would hardly be free to take off for The Congo or Latin America, but it may not strike her that something that needs doing only a few miles away is nearly as impossible for her. Whether it is a question of too few hours in the day, or too little money for baby-sitters, she may often find that her apostolic radius is limited to the home. If, however, she finds this to be more frustrating than challenging, then domesticity is probably not for her.

To a considerable degree, in the early years of motherhood, a woman sacrifices one sort of apostolic action for another: a wide though perhaps relatively shallow field of action in which many people can be reached is exchanged for a relatively narrow but intensive field of a few persons, her children. Still, it is difficult to agree with Father F. X. Arnold's oversimplification: "The kerygmatic activity in the home devolves primarily on the woman. . . . The mother, more than the father, decides the atmosphere of the home, including the religious atmosphere. It is the latter which fundamentally decides the religious development of the child by means of unconscious assimilation. . . . It is neither school nor public life that stamps and informs a person's character as much as the home. This above all is the place for the woman's kerygmatic apostolate, that is, for spreading a living faith."[15]

However, Father Arnold does go on to say that a "woman should not restrict herself to the apostolate of the home."[16] The very nature of lay life, situated in the world, suggests involvement in some sort of direct action, however limited, rather than complete withdrawal.

In short, marriage as a vocation is a rather untidy proposition. It seems neither to exclude contemplation and direct apostolic activity, nor to make either of them particularly easy. It has its own proper focus, the lifelong commitment to one's partner and to the presumably less than lifelong task of raising one's family, but it takes in slices of other kinds of life as well. It is a mistake to approach it as one clearly defined sort of vocation when it opens up such diverse possibilities.

There is, of course, a core of commitment about which one can make definite statements: the central relationships to husband and children. In this area of the wife and mother's vocation, it is difficult to single out legitimate options. A mother may, of course, quite reasonably feel that her vocation as wife and mother need not include a life-long dedication to doing the family laundry or making dinner seven nights a week. There is no necessary and sacred relationship between herself and a pile of mending or ironing,

[15] *Woman and Man*, pp. 79–80.
[16] *Ibid.*, p. 80.

if her energy and ability could be better used elsewhere, and if there is money available to pay someone else to do such chores. But there is a holy and inescapable relationship between herself and her children, no matter who or how talented she may be. The absolute prerequisite for the proper development of a child's spiritual and physical growth is that he be loved; and while the satisfying of this condition is the vocation of both parents, in the day-to-day, hour-by-hour life of the small child, it rests particularly with the mother.

One cannot measure precisely the effect of the presence or the absence of the atmosphere of love in any given life, but nevertheless it can often be seen as the decisive factor. Such a presence—or absence—for example, can be felt in the sensitive interpretation of Joan Erikson of the life of Eleanor Roosevelt, who out of the unhappiness and rebuffs of her childhood and young womanhood forged the deepest affirmative faith. "Could one not say," Mrs. Erikson writes, "that the young Eleanor and the mature woman she became were the product of an act of will—the will to be the daughter that her father had lovingly preordained, the daughter that would make him proud? This deep love for her father," she continues, "and her conviction that she was beloved and that much was expected of her was surely the source of the inner strength which upheld her and made it possible for her to transcend her misfortunes."[17]

This father, who was banished from her home because of his alcoholism when she was only eight, and who saw her only infrequently until his accidental death two years later,

[17] "Nothing to Fear: Notes on the Life of Eleanor Roosevelt," in *Daedalus*, Spring, 1964, pp. 797–798.

nevertheless had succeeded in giving her the glance of love, the glance that made her someone. But the absence of such a glance on her mother's part also slanted her development in its own way. It was an absence almost like a mysterious organic deficiency, which stunted one side of her growth irremediably. Eleanor Roosevelt could become "someone" —even a great someone—but not a person who could be comfortable in her own motherhood. "Her relationship with her mother," Mrs. Erikson writes, "at least in later child-hood, was certainly not one of loving mutuality . . . the daughter could not learn from the mother how to become the loving and caring mother of her own children. She writes of her own mothering, 'I never had any interest in dolls or in little children and I knew absolutely nothing about handling or feeding a baby. . . .' Writing in later life, she deplored this lack of training and understanding and expresses the wish that she had taken over the upbringing of her children herself. 'Had I done this,' she says, . . . 'my subsequent troubles would have been avoided and my children would have had far happier childhoods.' . . . In her story she emphasizes how strongly she felt her responsibility for her children's welfare, how dutifully she cared for them when ill or injured, but little joy or even satisfaction in mothering shines through."[18]

Strictly speaking, therefore, it is the quality of the re-lationships within the family that is the heart of the wife and mother's vocation, no matter what her particular cir-cumstances and abilities. Her response to the people en-trusted to her by God *is* her response to her calling by God,

[18] "Nothing to Fear," pp. 795–796.

her vocation. Her husband, her children, are the signs of God's particular providence.

In starting with what one can say generally about the vocation of the married laywoman, however, one almost inevitably finds oneself back with what is profoundly individual. Rather than some sort of abstract vocation to marriage and motherhood, there is a vocation to a life in Christ with this particular husband, and the children that come from their special love, with the unpredictable and unique stamp of God's design upon them. Nevertheless, vocation, when one speaks of it on the individual level where it belongs, is not exhausted by these particular relationships and by this one occupation of housewife and mother. The idea of vocation is both larger and more precise. It includes the totality of each woman, all that she comes to understand over many years as being herself, her identity. Moreover, this may be an identity in which much is included that is quite irrelevant to her daily work of making a home.

Seen from another angle, the stamp of uniqueness on each vocation is placed there by God, and is there for a particular purpose. In this sense, one really speaks of vocation as "mission."[19] Mission and vocation are the same reality, mission as it exists in the mind of God, vocation as the individual perceives it. Implicit in this perception is an obligation which is both exact and profound. There is not a housewife and mother's vocation, nor even, to make it more specific, a vocation in this particular decade in America for the Catholic married woman with a higher education. There

[19] See Hans Urs von Balthasar, *Thérèse of Lisieux*, Sheed and Ward, New York, 1957, p. xii.

are as many vocations as there are individual women. There is no easy way for the individual to find her vocation in the servile imitation of some pre-ordained pattern. The generalities that can be proffered about a lay or married woman's vocation give lines of direction, but they are no substitute for the painstaking, sometimes painful, work of discovery.

At this point, one cannot help speculating on the resemblances between working out a "life plan" and finding one's individual vocation. Both take into account the individual woman's needs and abilities. Both encompass "love and children and home,"[20] but stretch beyond these to include the whole sweep of a lifetime and the wisest use of all one's energies. There seems to be no particular virtue in excluding "planning" from the working out of one's individual vocation, no special merit in jolting blindly from one stage of life to the next, wasting time and talents. The "life planner" and the woman trying to use the virtue of prudence in working out her vocation may therefore look very much alike. Yet, despite the resemblances, they simply are not the same.

Perhaps the main difference is that the woman with a "life plan" is not so much finding her way of life as making it. She initiates the plan, and although she may be obliged by circumstances to modify it in this way or that, the goal itself, the "lifelong commitment to an art or science, to politics or profession,"[21] cannot possibly come into question. Mrs. Friedan admiringly describes the "pioneers" among life-planners in this way: "They had problems, of course, tough ones—juggling their pregnancies, finding nurses and

[20] Friedan, The Feminine Mystique, p. 338.
[21] Ibid., p. 348.

housekeepers, having to give up good assignments when their husbands were transferred. They also had to take a lot of hostility from other women—and many had to live with the active resentment of their husbands. . . . It took, and still takes, extraordinary strength of purpose for women to pursue their own life plans when society does not expect it of them. However, unlike the trapped housewives whose problems multiply with the years, these women solved their problems and moved on."[22] The life-planner, after all, is not trying to carry on a dialogue with someone else about the nature of her plan, although she may have to spar a little with the "active resentment" of her husband. But the very point of a vocation, is that it involves some kind of dialogue with God and with those who are close to oneself—not a once-and-for-all decision, rigidly held to with "extraordinary strength of purpose." It is an unfolding process of prayer and reflection on the changing circumstances that manifest God's intentions.

A vocation, unlike a life plan cannot be deduced simply by a careful study of the nature, abilities, and interests of the person concerned. Although these enter into the vocation, they do not determine it in any way that can be safely predicted. Those jogs and drastic alterations in circumstance that can be so exasperating to the life-planner—the husband's unexpected transfer, the loss of a housekeeper or the long illness of a child, or even the opening up of some quite unforeseen opportunity—are the strokes with which God sketches the whole picture of a vocation, perhaps altering one's original plan quite out of recognition. The strokes may

[22] *Ibid.*, p. 376.

be delicate, and almost unnoticeable. A woman, for instance, who has always worked with children in her spare time, finds that circumstances seem to be increasingly putting older people in her path who are in need of her help, and her gift for spontaneous enjoyment of other people is gradually drawn into a wholly unexpected channel. But whether the alteration is delicate or almost brutal, it goes on.

The woman with a vocation, unlike the life-planner, rarely sees the proposed shape of her life with certainty. While she may see that a certain strength of purpose is necessary to carry through even the most provisional of plans for its shaping—the forces of sheer inertia being what they are—her plans are provisional, for their fundamental requirement is that they fit into the larger design of God, whose outlines she cannot see. Being oneself, in the fullest sense, is not usually a matter of being true to the self grasped in a single moment of insight, but rather a gradually unfolding process with its share of surprises.[23]

In the idea of vocation as dynamic and gradually unfolding, strength of purpose and wisdom in planning are not expendable, but they yield first place to another quality, an openness and suppleness to the will of God. Without this openness, such strength can turn to a self-glorifying rigidity and the best of plans can go perversely astray. "Unless the Lord builds the house, those who build it labor in vain" (Psalm 127, 1).

This openness to the contingent is not a matter of passivity, of letting events big and little roll over one as "God's will," with no attempt made to shape or direct them. Rather it takes self-determination at its face value, with all

[23] Josef Pieper, *Prudence*, Pantheon, New York, 1959, p. 57.

the implications of forethought and effort, of purposeful, prudent choice that this value implies. But all the forethought, the effort, the planning have their beginnings in and must constantly return to an attitude, which is basic, of inner attentiveness to the will of God. This is the fundamental attitude of creature to Creator, from Abraham's "Here am I, Lord, at your command" to Mary's "Be it done unto me according to thy word"; whether it takes the form of religious obedience or the inner suppleness of mature self-determination.

As an example of what this whole question of an individual's unfolding vocation involves, one might take the crucial and emotion-charged question of "responsible parenthood." There is certainly no need to stress that it *is* crucial. The many articles, letters, statements, and books on various aspects of family planning have only brought to the surface the expression of a problem which has existed for many years. No other issue so dramatically affects not only the quality of family life, but the relationship of Christian family values to secular society, and of parents to the authority of the Church.

Mrs. Friedan has, in her own way, stated the "secular case." "There are women," she has said, "whose abilities are peculiarly suited to the mothering of babies. Instead of having baby after baby when our society has no room for so many babies, such a woman could find a lifelong fourth dimension by providing a new kind of professional baby care for mothers whose abilities lie elsewhere."[24]

This kind of heartless altruism—and plain disregard of a number of facts—naturally calls for reproof. Unfortunately,

[24] "Woman: The Fourth Dimension," p. 53.

the proposed "counter-attack" has too often been as rigid
and as antipersonalist as the planned-parenthood approach.
The assumption of the parents of large families, or their
defenders, is too likely to be that parents of two or three
children are calculating hedonists, whose value judgments
are accorded in equal measure to children, color television,
Cadillacs, and trips to Europe. What is an urgent requisite
on both sides of the argument is a greater respect for each
individual mother and father's uniquely personal vocation
to "responsible parenthood." This responsibility should not
be gauged in its success according to whether the family is
large, medium-sized, or small. The whole idea of planning
a family is so embedded in the vocations of both husband
and wife that it cannot, under normal circumstances, be
decided arbitrarily. There are no rule-of-thumb answers, because what is right from an economic or religious point of
view can be wrong from a medical or psychological point of
view. All generalizations, the radical as well as the secure,
ultimately become subject to the rigorous assessment of the
parents' own particular capabilities and circumstances. The
large family and the small family alike can be a blessing and
a great happiness, or a miserable existence and the source
of chaos and downfall.

The married couple's assessments and reassessments of
their situation are part of the attempt to carry out the mission entrusted to each individual by God. How large a part
of this mission these assessments are, neither the husband
nor the wife can ever know. When a young woman enters
upon her married life, she does not know whether it will be
long or short, whether she will have no children, few children, or many. She begins in uncertainty, if not in intention,

at least in the realization of the intention. The larger share of her life may be in widowhood, or perhaps her special charisma lies outside the confines of her family. Even so, however, her operative preparation for her vocation must assume that it will relate in some direct way to her marriage and motherhood, or rather, to put it negatively, that it will not be totally unrelated to her married life.

An attitude which takes all possibilities into account and refuses to pre-judge God's intentions is certainly not any evasion of the responsibilities of one stage in life, on the ground that something more important may be just over the horizon—in one's promising middle age, for instance. A genuine response to God's calling is always *now*, not at some indefinite or even precise future time. To respond means to be deeply engaged in this stage, this moment, almost as if it alone were to be decisive; and yet to have a readiness, an openness for what may come next. To be involved in the present, to plan for the future, and yet at all times to remain pliant and receptive to God's intentions— this is the truly difficult but necessary task. In effect, it attempts to combine the wholehearted *now* of the sacrament of the present moment, the prudent eye to the future of a provisional "life plan," and the sort of suppleness to the unplanned hazards and opportunities of that future, that keeps one's "outlines dim and misty on that side."[25]

Above all, there must be the continuous flow of response. Engagement in life does not mean clinging to or even anticipating any one moment or phase of experience as if it

[25] Henry David Thoreau: "In view of the future or possible, we should live quite laxly and undefined in front, our outlines dim and misty on that side." *Walden*, p. 289.

alone were the climax of life's meaning. It makes little difference whether one fastens upon innocent childhood, first love, the intellectual delights of college days, the experience of childbirth, or the joys of having children. Each one of these, intensely lived and felt, can be a word of God for the individual. If it is clung to, as if it were the only word or the last word, it becomes a dead letter. The possibility of communication with God through the whole flow of life has been closed off.

Once again, as in so many other matters, the intensity and openness of a lifelong response to God's calling is not a matter that only affects the individual woman. By choosing marriage and motherhood, she has laced her life deep with that of others, and indeed with the problems of a new generation.

The relationship of her slackened sense of vocation to the life of her husband is obvious. From being partner with her husband, she turns to dead weight, if the vital response to life suddenly and inexplicably drains away. If it goes in middle life, because her supposed "vocation" seemed to her to be irrevocably bound up with the years of young motherhood (and not very closely bound to him), he will be faced with the frustrating task of trying to pump or cajole some semblance of life into a middle-aged stranger. If it disappears even earlier, a too fragile sense of self and of vocation crumbling under the demands of the "distracted" life, then the prospects of preserving in the marriage something more than a veneer of busyness, or perhaps a desperate dependence, are not too hopeful.

Less apparent, perhaps, but just as critical, is the effect on the next generation. The mother who loosens her own grip on life, loosens the grip of her children. For them, she is not only in very large part their present—and a person who is not fully alive is cheating them of the present that could be—but she is also a visible expression of their future. Not only will the mother be the middle-aged woman that they must half-guiltily turn to or tear away from, but she is also the embodiment of what they might one day be—or marry. In effect, she is saying that this is what life really amounts to for a woman: a long spurt of energy, of preoccupation with family, and then all at once the crumbling away of an old façade.

In this age of rapid and perpetual change, an older generation may not be able to offer a younger generation very much in the way of specific practical advice. In ten years, perhaps less, everything from job opportunities to housekeeping techniques may be unbelievably transformed. But what the parents can give, or fail to give—is a sense that the purpose, the springs of life do not suddenly dry up long before life itself has ended. A sense of purpose maintained, of vocation continued—to the edge of death—is something owed not just to oneself, but to one's family as well: "Any span of the life cycle lived without vigorous meaning, at the beginning, in the middle, or at the end, endangers the sense of life and the meaning of death in all whose life stages are intertwined."[26]

[26] Erik H. Erikson, *Insight and Responsibility. Lectures on the Ethical Implications of Psychoanalytic Insight*, W. W. Norton, New York, 1964, p. 133.

VII

Leisure and Education

One of the recurring themes in the debate over the American housewife, whether she is seen to be trapped, urged to be creative, or thought a contemplative, is the insistence on the importance of higher education. It is viewed as the "key to the trap"[1] which can save the housewife from the dangers of the feminine mystique, and at the same time as the jewel in the apron pocket[2] of the woman who delights to stay at home. The Christian woman who wishes to exercise "a deep and widespread influence upon others" is reminded of her solemn obligation "to acquire the very best technical training";[3] and the mother who is satisfied to limit her influence to her own children is reminded with equal gravity that "she can't be too educated."[4]

Education is certainly no necessary entrée to cooking,

[1] Betty Friedan, *The Feminine Mystique*, p. 357.

[2] Phyllis McGinley, *Sixpence in Her Shoe*, p. 16.

[3] John Tracy Ellis, "The Catholic Laywoman and the Apostolate of Our Time," Address to the National Council of Catholic Women, November 6, 1962.

[4] Solange Hertz, *Searcher of Majesty*, p. 95.

cleaning, and child care. As professional training for work outside the home, a woman's education—if it were not in stenography or the like—is likely to be irrelevant or obsolescent by the time she goes to work. And yet the usual assumption is that, if a housewife wishes to save her children from her own destructive ignorance, or occasionally rise above banality, or overcome the worst hazards of discontinuity, what she needs is a college education.

At the same time, however, there is an undercurrent of unease as to the real need or effectiveness of education in a woman's life. A symptom of this unease is the recent movement to restructure women's higher education as "continuing education," rather than as a single block of years, early in life, leading to one or more degrees. In part, this piecemeal acquisition of courses or degrees by married women approaching or already in middle age is simply a pragmatic response to specific problems. One is the current teacher shortage, which will have to be met in large part by drawing on the women who have been dropping out of college to marry early. To a lesser degree, continuing education in some fields is also a response to the changes in our knowledge which force retraining even of those who have worked persistently in a given field.

Nevertheless, these matters are only the most obvious aspects of what appears to be a reëxamination, or redesigning, of women's higher education. This redesigning is not altogether encouraging. One grants that the vision conjured up of middle-aged women painstakingly accumulating credits for a teaching certificate may be somewhat dismaying to those who do not want to see women's education pushed in the same illiberal and utilitarian direction as men's. Nor is one cheered by the fact that even this aspect of continuing education as job-training or re-tooling is beyond the grasp of many of the older women who are attempting it.[5] Still, even in the name given to what may sometimes be rather dreary enterprises, there is an attempt to come closer to the notion of education as a sustained presence in the married woman's life. More significantly, it is bringing together, however inadvertently, two things which should really be operating as a single agent, education and leisure.

Of the two, leisure is habitually given less attention than education, and yet it would be possible to make a strong case for its being the true shaping force in the married woman's life. In the long run, her use or abuse of the free time available to her is far more significant than the number of years spent in higher education, or the degrees she has acquired. It is probable that the difference between an increasing apathy and automatism in the housewife—whether she sees herself as trapped or relatively content—and a sustained openness to life, lies in the little-explored area of leisure time.

Perhaps too often women forestall exploring the possibilities of their leisure time in the feeling that it is inappropriate, even somewhat satirical, to associate the spacious word "leisure" with their own distraction-filled

[5] Esther Raushenbush, director of the Center of Continuing Education at Sarah Lawrence College, has noted of older women: "They feel lost, and at this stage of their lives if they have made no plans it is hard to help them find an educational design for a new occupation . . . women in their later forties pose a sizable problem." "Second Chance: New Education for Women," *Harper's*, October, 1962, p. 150.

lives. The whole notion of leisure as something which is quite apart from the world of work, and not just a pause or a break, "a link in the chain of utilitarian functions . . . made for the sake of work,"[6] may be quite alien to them. Instead, they have come to know leisure in its counterfeits: the momentary diversions such as the morning coffee break, the afternoon nap, a day of shopping pressed between weeks of work, a glance through a magazine while the children are resting, the cocktail party, a dinner out. These are not manifestations of leisure, they are merely means to keep working—intended, as Walter Kerr has summarized the matter neatly, simply to keep "the battery running at an even purr."[7]

Admittedly, there are few sizable vacant blocks of time in the day or week of the mother of young children, even for diversion. Time which is genuinely left to her choice, what might be called discretionary time, is usually rather hard to come by. She need not follow a precise, hour-by-hour schedule, but all that this really means is that, apart from such regularly recurring chores as breakfast, dinner, and the baby's feedings, she can arrange the necessary work flexibly. There is nothing really "discretionary" about a bucket of dirty diapers, a pile of unironed laundry, or a row of unfilled formula bottles. All the time savers, the packaged foods, the clothes that need no ironing, may only mean a more manageable work load, not a real increase in leisure.

Still, however fluctuating and tenuous its existence may

[6] Josef Pieper, *Leisure, The Basis of Culture*, Pantheon, New York, 1952, p. 56.
[7] *The Decline of Pleasure*, Simon and Schuster, New York, 1962, p. 142.

seem, some discretionary time is available even in the busiest years of raising a family. By the stage in life when a housewife's children have entered school, it is likely to be almost annoyingly in evidence, and within a few more years, it can overwhelm the woman who has not learned what to do with it. Certainly, at all stages leisure is more available to those women who value it enough to search for it deliberately, than to those who see its importance as negligible, and who would regard working for free time as a contradiction in terms.

Perhaps the most time-honored expedient of the determined woman is to make use of the children's nap time, whether or not the children happen to be sincerely interested in sleeping, but this by no means exhausts the possibilities open to her. If an overcrowded home or hyperactive children mean that there are no quiet times in the day other than an occasional lull between storms, she may be able to manufacture longer blocks of time, perhaps once or twice a week. Some of the means to this end, such as part-time household help or a regular baby-sitter, involve both money and the presence of people in the community competent for such work. In the absence of one or both, one solution is the cooperative pooling of services by like-minded mothers in arrangements varying from the cooperative nursery school or baby-sitting service involving a large community group, down to the more or less regular but informal agreement between two or three mothers.

Another possibility which some women have attempted to implement is to try to confine these expedients to the family circle, and persuade one's husband to take over some child care and other domestic duties in *his* discre-

tionary time. In cases where husbandly talents and inclinations do not make him wholly "unsubstitutable," this
might seem like a tempting solution. Many fathers and
their children could well be spending more time together,
although much of the value of this time lies in the very
fact that the two parents are not interchangeable, and
that the children are not simply getting more of the same.
Nevertheless, dependence on a sort of "split-shift" arrangement in order to get sizable blocks of free time
would seem to risk cutting dangerously into the rather
brief time together that most husbands and wives already
share. However smothering total family togetherness may
become, a carefully worked-out system of apartness would
hardly seem like an improvement.[8]

Free time, in any case, whatever the means may be for
acquiring it, is not a luxury but a necessity. Even a seemingly negligible slice of the day, running at right angles
to routine occupations, can keep a woman in touch with
herself, with God, with the world outside her home, and
even with the family itself. Conditions under which
mothers cannot snatch any such time for themselves—or
are too exhausted to use it when it comes—should be
recognized for what they are, simply inhuman. Even so,
however, the mere presence of free time does not in itself
mean that one can thereby find leisure.

One could say, for instance, that generally the basic use
of leisure in the housewife's distracted life is to keep
inner and outer lines of communication open; these

[8] This is an obvious point of difference with Sidney Callahan's
approach in The Illusion of Eve (Sheed and Ward, New York,
1965), as set forth on pages 141–143. The difference is based on
the more fundamental disagreement with her urging of an "androgy-
nous . . . ideal for married Christians." P. 96.

would include reading, reflection, prayer, adult conversation, and the pursuit of whatever aspects of her "direct" work for the world she can reasonably handle. But even if these generalities are granted as true, there is the major difficulty of applying them in the right way at the right time. There is the woman whose use of free time results in the gentle dissipation of whatever powers of concentrations her scattered daily life has left her. She reads—but she feels that her run-down intellectual condition demands "light reading" as a sort of soft diet. Her work outside her home depends on which committee reaches her first, and it is likely to consist in fund-raising or bazaar-promoting.

At the opposite extreme is the woman who, while conscientiously limiting herself to the scraps of time available, tensely demands of them an impossible productivity. Given half an hour a day, she is determined to write a novel.

But the necessity for using free time with more intelligence and respect raises the question of education. We have already pointed out the almost accidental combination of the two in "continuing" education. It may, of course, only substitute a rather narrow if purposeful activity for various forms of diversion, but quite often it seems to move beyond this towards that greater fulfillment of being, the sharpening of vision that a genuine use of leisure should bring. A rather fuzzy life may begin to come back into focus.[9] What seems to be happening in these cases is that the broken connection between education and leisure

[9] Some rather exuberant remarks of reactivated housewives can be found in such articles as "Housewives on Campus: I Feel Alive Again," by Bernard Asbell, *McCall's*, November, 1963; and "I Went Back to College," by Barbara O'Neill, *Redbook*, November, 1963.

is being mended, and what one sees is not a new woman but a woman restored to herself. The whole key to the success of continuing education is that it carries on what has already been established in earlier years. The woman who has never learned to study, never tested out her interests and abilities over a wide range of possibilities, never really come alive intellectually in the years before her marriage, is at a marked, often a crushing disadvantage. Fitting even a modest schedule of study into the distracted life is difficult enough, without having to learn what study is.

It would be oversimplifying matters, of course, to say that only the woman with a higher education can be expected to cope with the problems of leisure. There are some young women who acquire nothing more from four years of college than a rather spotty patina of sophistication—perhaps also a husband—and a smaller number who do a rather good job of educating themselves. Still, there are more than a few indications that a liberal education will tend to produce the flexibility, the inventiveness, the discipline that is demanded.

Certainly, the absence of these qualities is marked in the approach to life of many women who have not had such opportunities. One study of the workingman's wife reports that, characteristically, "she has little interest, energy, or skill to explore, to probe into things for herself. . . . She has little inclination or training to stand back at some distance from herself to reassess her situation in large terms. . . . Mental activity is arduous for her . . . and she tends to experience discomfort and confusion when faced with ambiguity or too many alternatives."[10]

[10] Rainwater, et al., Workingman's Wife, p. 59.

On the positive side, we could say with some assurance that there is a sporting chance that the college graduate will emerge as a reader, and that during the years of relative isolation as a young mother, the questions of whether and what she reads are highly, almost disproportionately important. If there is little or no chance in her life for more than occasional or casual contacts with adults other than her husband, and for a range of experience outside the home that might nourish an authentic religious faith, or stimulate her mind, reading must often become the substitute for a more balanced kind of life.

If reading is to keep open her lines of communication, it can neither be second-rate nor one-sided. A conscientious policy of nothing but "spiritual reading" or Catholic books, for instance, would be a mistake, no matter how excellent the particular books might be. Unless she keeps the range of her reading wide, she may soon find that her college-acquired opinions and facts are as chillingly intact as if she had buried them in a time capsule. More than this, at certain times in her life, reading, together with prayer for others, may be all that remains to bridge past and future action in maintaining an attitude of concern and commitment. If she is to fight off the creeping onset of the kind of middle-class morality to which the married woman seems particularly subject, she must read deeply in works that are concerned with the *saeculum*, with this time, this place.

Without reading, many of the other uses of leisure, reflection, conversation, and prayer would be the poorer. Theoretically, for instance, reflection can be stimulated by almost anything: a small child sloshing around in a bath, a guinea pig's insatiable appetite, even—for a Solange Hertz—

the contents of a dustpan. But most women, whose minds are taking in a little Dr. Spock and *Woman's Day*, will simply dry the baby, feed the guinea pig, and dump the dustpan without a single ripple of thought emerging. These women need the vitality of another mind, or perhaps just the raw material of information, to prod their own minds into action. Then again, the reading woman may spare her husband the painful necessity of bringing home a little intellectual stimulation every night, like the hunter bringing in a rabbit for the stew pot.[11] In any event, she will have something to add to the stew. Not least of the values reading brings into her life may be its contribution to prayer. For a woman to whom reading is as natural as breathing, some sort of meditative reading might make prayer possible, even when attempts at formal meditation without such an anchor would degenerate uncontrollably into grocery lists or speculations as to what the children in the next room were doing so quietly.

Granted the importance of reading in the use of discretionary time, it is still not all-important. As more free time becomes available to a woman over the course of years, she seldom becomes a full-time reader, unless a particular line of work such as editing or research demands it. It would seem reasonable to suppose, moreover, that the advantages in relation to leisure of spending some years in college would extend further than an appetite for books.

Dorothy Dohen has made the rather uncommon sugges-

[11] Lucious F. Cervantes has remarked: "The mental interchange of mature monogamy could be facilitated by the husbands if they would make a conscious point of bringing home a humorous and an important event from their business day." *Marriage and the Family*, p. 362.

tion that there should be experiences during the college
years both in the teaching of formal subjects such as poetry
and outside the classroom which would encourage the acquiring of a contemplative spirit.[12] Difficult as this is to plan
or program in the presence of so many curricular and extra-
curricular pressures, it is precisely this knowledge of how to
spend unpressured moments, to be inwardly quiet and at-
tentive, that will vitalize her use of leisure in later years.

Indeed in the development of such a spirit, a great deal
more than the use of leisure is at stake. There is really no
point in talking about an unfolding vocation for a married
woman if event after event simply rolls over her, with no
attempt on her part to bring these events into the light of
God's presence and reflect on them. More than this, one
would hope that in married life, this capacity for solitary reflection would extend itself into the shared reflection, the
quiet reassessment that both husband and wife need in
order to keep in touch with the way their lives and the
whole life of the family seem to be taking shape. Not only
will this be necessary for the inwardness of family life, but
for the family's relationship to the community around
them. Certainly, there is no one Christian pattern for such
a relationship on which a family can readily fall back. There
may be types of family vocations, but, if so, they are at least
as diverse as those which distinguish Trappists from Jesuits
or Franciscans from Benedictines. Each couple must assess
for themselves which of the many demands made on that
elusive entity "the Christian family" are right for them,
there and then. Do they go back to the land, stir up the
suburbs, or work to stabilize a racially changing neighbor-

[12] *Women in Wonderland*, pp. 245–247.

hood? In these and countless other questions, they must summon up enough inner silence to really hear the choices —"Love *listens* to the particular situation and opens the mind to the creative possibilities before us."[13]

Undoubtedly, a contemplative spirit is *not* the attribute most commonly expected of the college-educated woman, even in relation to her free time. A certain degree of specialization, and of technical proficiency in that specialization, would be a more usual expectation, with the accompanying hope that her free time would be very largely used in keeping that specialty alive. A taste for reading and the contemplative spirit are all very well, but the minimum return on these very expensive years of education would be the young woman's ability to do some one thing competently, and her tenacity in continuing to pursue it, at least on a part-time basis, after marriage.

Precisely because the maintenance of this sort of continuity can be such a worthwhile use of "discretionary time," and one which we will explore at greater length in the next chapter, it seems necessary to point out that it is not a uniform pattern for the fusing of education and leisure. Too many women simply pick the wrong field of specialization in their college years, and it would be a disaster for them to tie themselves to these particular competencies as lifelong commitments. A mature woman may see her one-time college major as thoroughly irrelevant to her present interests and capacities. Quite possibly, it was simply a desperate choice between several equally plausible and uncompelling alternatives, and it has taken her many

[13] Bernard Murchland, C.S.C., "The Ethics of Possibility," Introduction to *The Authentic Morality* by Ignace Lepp, Macmillan, New York, 1965.

years and some wrong turnings to find her real direction. Nor can one expect too much of even the valid specialization before marriage if it is extremely narrow. There is little point in being a competent marine biologist if one's husband's occupational specialty keeps him in Denver.

Indeed, one may have the liveliest regard for competence in any work for or in the world which married women may undertake and still feel that the polishing of a particular ability is not the central task of women's higher education, at least on the undergraduate level. Far more important for the sort of complex and ever-changing situations in which married women are likely to find themselves is the development of the many-sided mind, the ability to sift possibilities, to create new solutions, to adapt and redirect one's energies. At its best, higher education does seem to encourage this sort of development, demanding a growth in independent thought and autonomy, and even at more mediocre levels it does to some degree open out new perspectives and avenues of approach. By and large, it is the educated woman who will be the innovator in the use of her free time, and this may be particularly noticeable in her approach to community activities. She is not altogether immune to passive, dues-paying membership, but there is at least a reasonable chance that she will go beyond this and look for the constructive possibilities in the situations at hand.[14]

Furthermore, there is at least some ground for hope that

[14] Concerning her former college classmates, Betty Friedan remarks that "community activity almost always had the stamp of innovation and individuality, rather than the stamp of conformity, status-seeking, or escape." *The Feminine Mystique*, p. 359. Among the activities she mentioned were setting up cooperative nursery schools, teenage canteens and libraries in schools, new educational programs, working for desegregation of schools, and mental health clinics.

this freedom to act, this capacity for innovation, will have been tempered in the college years with some measure of discipline. Mere impulsiveness may be charming or irritating, depending on the age of the woman involved, but it seldom involves selecting the most appropriate solution. It may or may not represent untrammeled femininity or "woman's way," but if it does, then it is one of the functions of education for women to correct the bias of this kind of rampant and unpruned femininity. We suggested earlier that to be "all woman" with no development of "masculine" qualities is to be off balance. As Edith Stein has pointed out, the results of such an imbalance can be most unpleasant: "The personal tendency is usually unwholesomely exaggerated; on the one hand woman is inclined to be extravagantly concerned with her own person and to expect the same interest from others; this expresses itself in vanity . . . and an unrestrained urge for self-expression and communication. On the other hand we shall find an unmeasured interest in others which shows itself as curiosity, gossip and an indiscreet longing to penetrate into the intimate life of other people. The tendency towards wholeness easily leads her to frittering away her energy; it makes her disinclined to discipline her individual talents properly and leads to superficial nibbling in all directions. In her attitude to others it shows itself in a possessiveness far exceeding what is required by her maternal functions. Thus the sympathetic companion becomes the interfering busybody that cannot tolerate silent growth and thus does not foster development, but hinders it."[15] Far from accept-

[15] Quoted by Hilda C. Graef in *The Scholar and the Cross*, Newman, Westminster, 1955, p. 77.

ing this as the inevitable drift of feminine nature, Edith Stein points out that the "counterpoise in the natural realm is intellectual effort, work with ideas, or creative work with things, or work for the world at large; such concerns will keep a woman from attaching herself to the lives of those entrusted to her, from meddling and immoderate closeness."

Naturally, such a "counterpoise," to be effective, has to be exerted over a lifetime, and in the busy years of child-raising, the activities in leisure or discretionary time should be directed towards just such a balance. But the counterpoise is hardly likely to exist at all if it is not brought strongly into being in the years of preparation for marriage. In this regard, the "unfeminine" disciplines which force young women to deal with logic and abstractions—philosophy, metaphysics, mathematics, sociology—have a special if sometimes misunderstood function in women's education. As long as a real balance is kept, with a genuine respect for what is good in the allegedly feminine or intuitive way of approaching things, it is not a waste of time to make various efforts to get away from "the concrete, the personal, the particular."[16] It is simply an attempt to correct a bias that is no more of an asset to a woman than it is to a man, an inability to see the wood for the trees. Similarly, one can see that even the "irrelevant" major in college,

[16] Gerald Vann, O.P., *The Water and the Fire*, Sheed and Ward, New York, 1954: "The primary purpose . . . must surely be to educe and deepen the intuitive life of woman, her womanly wisdom. The time spent (or wasted) in school on chemistry or trigonometry would be better employed in opening to the girl, in a feminine way, the world of poetry, of the fine (and domestic) arts. . . ." P. 139.

which will not lead directly into an occupation in later life, provides a necessary growth in discipline, sets a standard for competent and fairly intensive work, and counteracts the inclination to intellectual nibbling.

One expects this kind of mental discipline from the years of higher education. It will be the groundwork for later work with ideas. But it does not seem excessive to expect some preparation for more active work for the "world at large" as well. A few colleges, Bennington and Antioch, for instance, have attempted to integrate practical work experience into the school year, guiding and evaluating the choice of work as part of the total educational process. But wherever this formal sort of integration is impossible, there should still be a diversity of opportunities offered informally, to be pursued on week-ends or during vacation periods. Some examples of such action would be the vacation projects in Appalachia, the work in the Freedom Schools and voter-registration drives in the South, the summer vacation enterprises of Amigos Anonymous in Mexico, and the tutoring of children in slum areas close to colleges throughout the country.

In some cases, these short-term commitments might lead directly to professional training or to the giving of a year or more after graduation to such movements as the Peace Corps, Papal Volunteers, the Grail, or a Catholic Worker House of Hospitality. Whether or not such an extended commitment is made at such an early stage in life, however, it might be expected to plant seeds of love, responsibility, and mission to a non-domestic world. Indeed, without some sort of seeding in actuality, it may be rather visionary to hope for a widespread harvest of

matured and active generosity among the middle-aged—
or a breaking-down of the fortress mentality of the individual housewife. In any case, it should provide, in a quite
practical way, a touchstone for evaluating the kind of
volunteer work typically available to the mother of school-
age children.

Without some previous contact with genuine needs and
her own capacity to meet them, a woman can well lose
the saving sense of when to say no. There is a certain
minimum level of coöperation which may be reasonably
expected of any able-bodied parishioner and mother of
school children. But beyond this minimum, she is obliged,
if only in the name of common sense, to subject all
requests to two brief tests: Is this job that I am being
asked to do worth doing in the first place? And, if it is,
am I the right sort of person to do it? Past experience
could supply a redeeming note of reality to both these
tests.

The whole bringing to bear of one's education upon the
use of leisure time should mean a constant effort of discrimination between those activities which pass and those
which "redeem" time. Quite often, for the educated Catholic woman, such discrimination in the past has simply
meant the elimination of all participation in school and
parish activities. Unless one lives in the dwindling number of parishes where the female laity are still firmly confined to bazaars and bingo, rummage sales and fashion
shows, this would seem to be a mistake. Usually, more
challenging opportunities already exist—or given some
tact and energy can be brought into being. One obvious
area would be work for the Confraternity of Christian

Doctrine. The woman who attempts teaching in this program may feel incompetent or overwhelmed, particularly if she happens to hit one of the more difficult age levels or teaching situations, but she is unlikely to think that the work is insignificant. In fact, her difficulties may, in some cases, lead her to the further step of suggesting changes in what is not yet a perfected program.

Confraternity work does not exhaust the possibilities for significant action on the parish level. If word of the various renewals, biblical, liturgical, and doctrinal, is to spread to the laity, this is going to mean much effort in the almost untouched field of adult reëducation and formation. Indeed, the whole area of schooling, both within and outside the parish, is so critical that it offers a whole range of possibilities. The parochial school or local Catholic high school is likely to be both over-crowded and under-staffed and financed, so that it could well use whatever type of part time voluntary help a particular women is best equipped to give, whether it be work with the library, foreign-language program, athletics, or correcting of tests and papers. At least equally worth-while would be the crossing of parish boundaries to work with a tutoring or pre-school program in the poorer areas of one's diocese.

If one takes it that "the world at large" means people, there are all sorts of things that can be done with and for people besides educating them—or selling them a book of raffle tickets. Sometimes an existing organization within the parish, neighborhood, or diocese, such as a Christian Family Group or Legion of Mary, a House of Hospitality, an inter-racial or political organization, will suggest and channel one's particular approach. Those who have begun a particular kind of work in college years may find the means to carry it on, part-time, in their own community. But even in situations where existing organizations are few, or ossified, a real attentiveness to the needs of others can open opportunities for the basic gifts of concern and companionship. With a baby in an orphanage or hospital ward, something as simple as being held and talked to with love is the very gift of life itself. For an older person, bedridden at home or in an institution, or for the mentally ill, the gift of interest and concern may be almost as basically the difference between life and a living death of loneliness.

The educated woman is frequently urged to add a third and decisive test to her free time activities beyond those or their intrinsic worth and her ability to do them. Of each commitment she must ask whether or not it fits into the over-all continuity of her "life plan." Is this volunteer work, for instance, a dead-end, or will it lead directly or indirectly to work that merits professional recognition, status, and pay?

From a Christian point of view, such a test has an unpleasant air of calculation. One can hardly imagine weighing the potentialities for continuity against the pressing needs of one's neighbor. Nevertheless, a distinction between the generous discontinuous work and the calculating act based on a lifetime continuity is somewhat unreal. In the generosity itself of the seemingly isolated activity, the depth of a commitment made to a person or a cause outside the immediate domestic world, a line of continuity between present and future is maintained. Indeed, in the rather fragmented time at the disposal of the woman who still has small children at home, it may well be the density of commitment in a particular activity which is critical, rather than its supposed place in an orderly scheme.

In the course of time, however, as a woman's children enter school, and the "extra life" comes almost perceptibly closer, she will find more impressive blocks of discretionary time at her disposal. With this increase, it is not niggling or ungenerous of her to try to find a more deliberate, a calculated plan for her free time. On the contrary, the really generous gift of self is bound to involve a very careful working out of her own particular pattern of vocation to the world.

VIII

The Committed Life

Of all the periods of a married woman's life, the transition phase, which ordinarily takes in most of her thirties and the early forties, is the most important from the point of view of choice. The way in which she chooses, either by deliberation or through default, to use the time at her disposal is considerably more significant than it was in the crowded early years of marriage, when the opportunities available were relatively meager; and when she was, rightly, almost totally involved in the life of her family. Although the range of choice open to her when her children have actually left home may seem to be greater, the capacity to choose and act significantly when that time has come is really created in the early years.

The whole balance of a woman's life, and her children's, is subtly changing throughout this transition period, even though the routine of daily life may not look very different from one year to another. The children's center of gravity is shifting from home and parents to school and friends. This is, in effect, the first stage of their departure. Both her children's need for a greater separateness and her own need for a counterweight in her life, a change in the channeling of her love and energy, will give real meaning to her apparently insignificant choices of this activity or that.

These are not, therefore, years for engaging in a multiplicity of superficial activities which keep a woman perpetually gliding across the surface of her life, nor even for various works in which she could be more deeply involved but which are at the same time random and undirected. On the contrary, this is preëminently the time for concentration on a "counterpoise" of serious work. Here there will be no instant professionalism. Indeed, it makes sense to think of this stage in life as one of apprenticeship in developing one's particular work in the world. In one's family life it is the continuation of an apprenticeship in love which may, in fact, receive its most realistic testing towards the close of this period. Certainly, in any case, growth in the capacity to give love within the family is a critical part of the over-all preparation of any work of love for the world. However, in very specific ways this time must also be one of training or retraining, and probably the time for taking the first steps in some definite line of work.

Ideally, a woman will already have a rather definite idea of what that work might be. The groundwork, moreover, should have been laid in her practical experience during and after college, and in her activities during the discretionary time of early marriage. However, many women will have taken advantage of neither time, so they will have to make a beginning by experimenting, testing out various possibilities, before they can make a choice. In different types of volunteer work, for instance, they might have to undergo the elementary business of finding out what they do well or badly, enjoy or simply endure. After several years spent mainly in the company of small children, they may need to become acquainted with their public selves and discover that their loquacity or silence, their diffidence, or even their panic, about taking on responsibility, is only a temporary symptom of reëntry.

The result of this testing out should be a more realistic assessment of her strengths and weaknesses. A woman who was generally attracted to some kind of work with children, might find after taking on a catechism class that she has a genuine bent for teaching, and decide to complete the necessary training through some form of continuing education. Or she might find that she was unable to handle more than three or four children together without chronic pandemonium, and turn her efforts to a type of work in which she would be dealing with only one child at a time —perhaps physical therapy or some kind of tutoring or counseling.

This sort of period of trial and assessment may be necessary, too, for the woman who gravitates towards a serious use of free time which is not directly oriented to some practical achievement, for the apprentice artist or musician, scholar or writer. She will usually find that for a time at least she must occupy a sort of no man's land between dilettantism or occupational therapy and work at a professional level. Over long periods of time she may not be able to point to the story or painting sold that could clear her of the charge of dabbling, and seem to justify the hours, sometimes the extra expense for household help or training, that she must put into this effort. Indeed, she may not be sure within herself whether she is simply in need of a centering activity in her life, as a condition of her ability to function as a whole and generous human being, or whether she is finding the main channel of a specific vocation in years to come. Need for an activity which is self-expressive and brings one "inner attentiveness" isn't necessarily linked to genuine ability. But time to produce a reasonable body of work, and professional criticism, may be needed to separate the perennial amateus from the future professional, and to distinguish an escape from a vocation. The Sunday painter or poet and the woman who will take her work more and more seriously both need a sustained effort at this time of life to probe for their own limits, and arrive at a reasonably realistic grasp of their own capacities.

In one sense, this period tests a woman's inner discipline, her capacity to plan rather than to follow the course of least resistance, to show responsibility in any part-time commitments that she undertakes, whether paid or voluntary, and to accept the tedious or highly demanding phases of any solitary interest that she pursues at home. Yet, far more is being tested than her ability to single out and pursue an occupational goal. On a natural level, she is being asked to find out for herself what it means to be "uniquely creative" without accepting a stereotyped masculine or feminine standard. As Erikson has remarked, it "is as yet unpredictable what the tasks and roles and opportunities and job specifications will be once women are not merely adapted to male jobs but when they learn to adapt jobs to themselves."[1] The working out of such an

[1] "Inner and Outer Space," p. 604.

adaptation that will truly suit her own nature, her situation, the totality of her vocation, is what is demanded of
her in these middle years of her life.

When we are speaking of the particular effort of an individual woman to pattern her life in a creative way, obviously we are not talking in terms of her finding a "feminine" rather than a "masculine" occupation to supplement
her role as wife and mother. It may very well be true that
in the over-all pattern, among women who are freely
choosing their own occupational designs (and this freedom
would have to include both a lack of pre-conceived notions
of "woman's work" and a very open choice of vocations),
the predominant tendency is to choose "feminine" rather
than "masculine" types of work. If we wish to generalize
about the over-all pattern of choice, therefore, we can also
validate and narrow it somewhat with Edith Stein's insight
that woman "tends towards the living and personal," and
that she is interested in the "dead thing, the 'object,' " not
for its own sake, but only "in so far as it serves the living."[2]
Indeed, it may also be true that at the highest levels of
achievement in certain fields, one sex will definitely pre-
dominate, even in the absence of overt discrimination. But
on the individual level, none of these considerations may
be of any real significance. If a woman's talent happens to
be mathematical, it would be utterly pointless to try to
convince her that she will be true to her feminine nature
by ignoring the "dead thing." She is as God made her, and
it is her business to develop what He gave her, with a fine
disregard for the alleged inclinations of the majority of her
sex.

The integration of this talent into her life as married

[2] Quoted in Graef, *The Scholar and the Cross*, p. 76.

woman and mother is what demands a genuinely feminine adaptation on her part. No matter how unusual or "masculine" her talent may be, its working out in the context of her daily life will be rather different from what it would be were she free to pursue it with the relative single-mindedness of the man or of the unmarried woman. In practical terms, being uniquely creative is going to involve choosing from, or even inventing, a whole range of variations on male-oriented work arrangements.

The most obvious area for adaptation is in the length of the working day outside the home. Part-time or shortened work schedules of one kind or another may not turn out impressive work loads, but they are the most obvious defense against neglect of the family and sheer exhaustion for the woman with children still at home. Paid part-time work open to women at present is often routine and unskilled, for example clerking in a department store during rush seasons, or selling cosmetics door-to-door; but if one has a skill that is in demand, this need not be true. Teaching is perhaps the most obvious instance, but a number of other fields of skilled work exist where a part-time schedule may often be possible, among them nursing, library, and social work.[3]

Simply on the level of time, it seems still more apparent that women who want to combine a profession of some kind with marriage will find any effort to prove that they can work in the same way as their male colleagues or competitors quite overwhelming. It is predicted that over "the next twenty years first-rate professionals will in most cases

[3] See Cooper, A Woman's Guide to Part-Time Jobs, pp. 37–39, 43.

be in such short supply that for them a 60- to 70-hour work week will be closer to the norm than 40."[4] Indeed, if women are intent on proving anything at all, it should be that they must have the right to make their contributions to the professions in their own way—with a high quality of work on a reduced time schedule.

Still another area for adaptations in the integrating of work for the world and home is the physical site of such work. Once again, it makes little sense for the mother with children still at home to try to fit herself into the current male pattern of widely separated home and work locations. Hours of commuting not only complicate an already crowded schedule, they make it almost impossible to give children the security of knowing that their mother is quickly available in an emergency. Indeed, the ideal would be work which is done either in the home or the immediate neighborhood. Some kinds of work are obviously more adapted to this kind of integration than others. There is nothing unusual about the notion of a home studio, of writing, or professional typing or dress-making in the home. There have also been a few fairly recent innovations in the cooperative efforts of a few women to set up "cottage industries" in their homes, pooling talents in such unexpected fields as textbook editing and computer programming. Such attempts to pool talents and resources may provide a new line of direction for women who find great difficulty in satisfying by themselves the demands of home and work when they suddenly pull in quite opposite directions. A business firm has no built-in provision for adapt-

[4] Donald N. Michael, The Next Generation, Vintage Books, New York, 1965, p. 123.

ing itself to such recurrent crises in its employees' home life. But with like-minded women, the situation is different: If "the working body has four heads, one or even two can be spared to meet family 'deadlines.' "[5]

Practically speaking, it will not always be possible for individual women to find the ideal or even approximately right adaptations of time and place that would meet their situations. Nevertheless, the chances of finding them will be infinitely improved if women can approach their work for the world unpretentiously, with a real sense of interior liberty. Without freedom from a nagging desire to prove and assert herself, to win status, or to get a grip on her identity, a woman is going to have the greatest difficulty in finding the way in which God apparently wants her to serve the world. It is hard enough to find the best way of doing a necessary job, without adding an obsessive concern for professional acceptance or for breaking down the barriers to female equality.

An unencumbered flexibility of this kind is important not only for the educated women who are approaching their "second lives," but for the society in which they are preparing to work. In forecasting various likely developments in this country over the next twenty years, one observer has remarked: "The poverty program, Peace Corps, and civil-rights movement presage increasing opportunities for subprofessionals in social service activities where no machine can replace face-to-face human exchange. Professionals, overwhelmed with tasks a sensitive, intelligent technician could do, will surrender them to the right kinds of people rightly trained. The status and education for

[5] Friedan, "Woman: The Fourth Dimension," p. 52.

these people is presently unclear, but a recognized need for them will steadily increase."[6]

It is reasonable to suppose that married women who no longer have heavy family responsibilities could make a real contribution in this area. The uncertainties of pay, status, training, and so forth, would not present the same difficulties to them as to married men who are obliged to count on a steady income. In "face-to-face" dealings with other people, moreover, a married woman speaks to the condition of the vast majority of the human race in the way that a single woman cannot. She knows what it is to bear children, worry and rejoice over them, work over long years with the marvelous and stubborn uniqueness of individuals—with no options about changing her job. All the growing up in love that motherhood has meant is at least as well worth offering to the world as the enthusiasm of youth—if she is willing to add to this the further discipline of necessary training.

Quite possibly, the place for the wholly untrained volunteer who brings little else but good will—and an infinite capacity for licking stamps—is disappearing. In any case, this sort of unfocused benevolence on the part of a woman is not going to fill her "extra" working life of perhaps twenty years. The need for persons who will add competence to love, and bring both to situations which offer little reward in the way of money or career certainly is not.[7] One example of this sort of area where the need for

[6] Michael, The Next Generation, p. 129.

[7] Maxine Davis, for instance, remarks that if "more women in middle life were to make voluntary service their new careers the philanthropic dollar would stretch much further. In 1959 alone Americans contributed $7 billion. Anywhere from 20 to 60 cents

workers is pressing but pay and status most uncertain is pre-school work with children in slum areas. These rather random and uncoördinated efforts in various cities are being "professionalized" as part of President Johnson's program for "the Great Society," but until recently they have depended largely on the initiative and personal concern of volunteers. More than this, as such pilot programs are expanded into a nation-wide, systematic effort, it is out of the labor pool of educated married women, willing to work for the world, that these new teachers must be drawn.

Putting the emphasis on service to the world rather than on status or career for Christian women in their middle age does not mean that they should all be volunteers. Some women must bring extra income into the family at this time of life, particularly if several children are passing through the expensive years of higher education. Others, because of a particular talent, may be, almost incidently, paid very handsomely for work which is genuinely and primarily one of service. What this emphasis does mean is that the real continuity of a married woman's "second life" of whatever duration, whether it be only a few years or several decades, must be built on a growth in love. The practical continuities of training and work which sustain previous interests are only means to maintain and develop this line of growth.

---

out of each of those dollars is paid out for professional services from executives to typists, from social case workers to the clerks who file all the records. These paid professionals are essential, but there are also plenty of women in the new leisured class who are or can easily become as competent as the salaried personnel." *Getting the Most out of Your Best Years*, p. 161.

The woman of middle age whose children have left home may find it somewhat exasperating to be told that "the time has come for her to think of old age, and so of death."[8] On the whole, she can probably think of more useful ways of spending the remaining years of her life than entering upon a sustained meditation on her coffin. Of course, a genuinely Christian understanding of what her old age and death should express is essential to the shaping of these middle years. If old age is foreseen, however dimly, as a time of self-centered preoccupations, then middle age can only be seen as a span from the purposeful to the purposeless.

There is no reason, in other words, to view old age as a time of "disengagement." The witness of many deeply Christian lives point in quite another direction. Often, there is in old age an almost visible intensification of love and concern, which has little or nothing to do with the degree of physical health and mobility. It is this idea of the inner dynamism of the Christian vocation which puts the "extra life" of the married woman, be it five years or twenty-five, into its true perspective. This period is not meant to be spent in the pursuit of ambitions that can only come to a more or less abrupt and cruel end or in a passive waiting for death. Nor is it simply the search for "a way out of the biologic complications"[9] now that reproductive life is com-

[8] Marc Oraison, *Man and Wife. The Physical and Spiritual Foundation of Marriage* (published originally as *Union in Marital Love*), Macmillan Paperbacks, New York, 1962; from his remarks on the "trauma" of "this very hard stage in life's conflict"; pp. 76–77.

[9] Helene Deutsch, in her massive interpretation of the psychology of women, speaks of the "thrust of activity" in the pre-climacterical life period which "expresses woman's protest, her

ing to an end, or for a new kind of life "lived in miniature" to balance psychological growth.[10] While it may, in an incidental way, accomplish both these latter aims, its inner meaning is the expression of a charity which grows without ceasing.

Generally speaking, we could say that the growth of love in these years will find its expression in spreading outwards from the home. The remaining family responsibilities in an ordinary household without children simply do not satisfy a "full-time" service of love. Certainly, there are exceptions, and it would be a mistake to think of these years as necessarily free from cares at home. A woman could not turn her back, for instance, on an invalid in the family, or an elderly, ailing parent, in order to rush out and "serve the world." There will be new relationships added during these years in most cases—sons- and daughters-in-law as well as grandchildren. Still, ordinarily, the time a woman spends within and outside the family may be almost the reverse of that in earlier years. Excepting one case, we could say that there will usually be less density and more scope to the relationships of love.

------

assertion that she is not merely a servant of the species, not a machine for bearing children, that she has higher brain centers and a complicated emotional life that is not restricted to motherhood. Thus she may succeed in actively finding a way out of the biologic complications." *Psychology of Women*, volume two, pp. 458–459.

[10] Dr. Esther Harding has observed: "It is by no means rare for a woman whose children have grown up to engage herself . . . in some kind of work in the world. . . . If they could recognize the subjective aspect of their adventure they would be content with a very modest external success. . . . Thus there is opened to her a second life, lived in miniature as it were, but capable none the less of carrying the opportunity for psychological growth which she missed through her former one-sidedness." *The Way of All Women*, p. 283.

The exception, of course, is the relationship between husband and wife. If there is some break in the intense meshing of life between mother and children, this should certainly not be true of the bond between the two parents. On the contrary, the "second life" is preëminently the time when husband and wife can become "reacquainted." No longer will there be the need to plot or struggle for a quiet evening or a week-end alone together. On the contrary, time with its plea for a deepened friendship will be present in abundance. If, in an almost panic reaction to this new depth in relationship, a woman fills the middle years with redoubled activities and appointments, so that intimacy is once again impossible, the most profound meaning of this part of life slips out of focus.

There is not some abstract ideal for middle age, as if it made no difference whether the woman in question were married or single, widowed, or a religious in vows. Nor can one assume that the state of marriage simply puts some negative restrictions on activity—that the married woman is not free, for instance, to travel extensively without her husband. Growth in charity for a wife, entering her "second life," is inextricably bound to growth in love for her husband, and this in turn should bring a deepened sensitivity to the ways in which she can be a fully complementary companion to him during this stage in her life.

Sometimes, as we have seen, this companionship and helping will include sharing extra financial burdens, and this will mean that a woman's vocation to the world will be channeled into paid rather than volunteer work—or perhaps into direct assistance in her husband's work. On the other hand, both husband and wife might find themselves free enough from family responsibilities to begin some new form of service to the world together. Not all lay missionaries need be young, single people, nor is it necessary to go any farther than the big central city areas in our own country to find persons in desperate need of personal help.[11] It is probable, moreover, that these people need, more than they do professional help from outside coming into their lives for a few hours a week, the continuity and sympathy that come from those willing to share life in the same neighborhood. Admittedly, not every married couple of middle age is suited to this particular kind of service to the world, but it is at least worth noting that this stage of life can provide a sort of freedom and flexibility which is infinitely more difficult to achieve when there are the needs of growing children to be considered.

If we are to speak meaningfully of the extra life which married women now typically live for many years after their children have grown and left home, it is necessary to emphasize what has been put forward too little, particularly in Christian thought in the past, namely, the importance of effective activity, of "positive healing action towards the world."[12] The terrible waste, past and present, of what women could offer if they only saw these years as part of the totality of their vocation, really demands such an emphasis. But it is important, too, that they realize that this life stage which may begin with a burst of activity

[11] In *My People is the Enemy* (Holt, Rinehart, New York, 1964), William Stringfellow suggests that if we wish to help the poor effectively, we must live with them; and this has, of course, been the *modus operandi* for many years of such movements as the Catholic Worker Houses of Hospitality.

[12] Rahner, *The Christian Commitment*, p. 57.

usually must end in a withdrawal into greater inwardness.

There are those who end their lives in an extended middle age, and die in full activity, but for many women the last stage in life will be something quite different, a time of life which, as Father LaFarge says, "exemplifies in countless ways a great principle of our existence: *the principle of growth-through-diminishment*."[13] Rather than reaching out to new activities and enterprises, they will face a time of stripping-down and cutting back.

Only an inner life of love can provide the final continuity of true "growth-through-diminishment" rather than the last flickering out of the fire of charity. In this respect alone, one sees the continuing need for setting aside some measure of time for true leisure, time for prayer and reflectiveness, to keep open the inner lines of communication with God and self during the years of direct service to the world. If life has remained all of a piece, because one's actions, no matter how seemingly scattered, have sprung from a sustained effort to find God's will and do it, then there will be strength left in old age to fight one's own latent forms of selfishness.

Old age almost certainly means doing less. The confinement of the young housewife to home and neighborhood may be exchanged for the walls of a single room. It may even bring the final "diminishment" that is the stripping away of her intellectual powers. But to the very last moment of conscious choice it should not mean being or caring less. If love fails, then even the most continuous life has been an extended arc of futility.

[13] *Reflections on Growing Old*, p. 28.

⚹ Conclusion

Edith de Rham, the author of a recent book on women, has casually remarked of the past history of her sex: "Women have been second-rate."[1] Should a woman tend to balk at this estimate, however, she may turn to the more perceptive observation of Virginia Woolf, that "There is no mark on the wall to measure the precise height of women. There are no yard measures, neatly divided into the fractions of an inch, that one can lay against the qualities of a good mother or the devotion of a daughter, or the fidelity of a sister, or the capacity of a housekeeper."[2]

Even so, though their judgments on women are not the same, Miss de Rham and Miss Woolf are agreed that women are being drawn by change beyond the unmeasurable personal sphere of wife, mother, housekeeper. Women may be carrying out more visibly, on a wider stage, activities which once belonged within the home, such as teaching and nursing, or expressing wholly new possibilities of the "quite possible She"; they may be handling this expansion of their activities wisely or wastefully—but the wholly private world, the family-centered lifetime for women, is disappearing.

[1] *The Love Fraud*, Clarkson N. Potter, New York, 1965, p. 304.
[2] *A Room of One's Own*, p. 148.

Perhaps the most striking manifestation of this change is the "second life" of married women, the probability that the years devoted mainly to raising their children will represent only a phase, a sizable fraction of their married lives, and that they will be faced with a second phase in their extended middle years, no longer centered on the family. This is the probability, the dominant life pattern for women in our society, and seems likely to be maintained for some years to come. Because such a pattern has neither been clearly envisioned nor taken very seriously in relation to the vocation of Christian married women, it has seemed to us worthwhile and even necessary to try to make the relationship clearer. A notion of vocation which stops for many women in mid-life is an absurd one.

Although there is reason to set out these two "lives" as sequences in time, in a characteristic life pattern, this may obscure their true significance. Certainly, present commentators on the two stages seem almost invariably tempted to weigh one "life" against another, and to chafe at this seemingly awkward distribution of women's years and talents. Depending on their view of woman's nature, they may be distressed that the conscientious mother should have to spend so many years of deferred fulfillment in domestic occupations, or saddened at the thought that a being whose obvious destiny and fulfillment is motherhood should have to linger on in the alien, arid occupations of a "second life." Somehow, the note of commiseration keeps creeping in.

If one takes a less single-minded view of women, if one is convinced, as we are, that they are neither wholly explicable in terms of motherhood, nor so similar to men that it is impossible to tell them apart without an anatomy

chart, then it seems that commiseration was never less
needed. Since women do seem to be more oriented than
men towards the care of children and the whole life of
the family, one need not take the years spent in child-
raising to be a rather unfair and wasteful division of labor
between the sexes. Since their potentialities are often not
wholly used in this aspect of their lives, moreover, it is not
unnatural to expect them to spend a good part of their
lives in preparing for and carrying out activities that have
nothing to do with mothering and housework. The present
untidy and often wasteful distribution of their lives, split
into various phases, divided between multiple roles and
many-channeled activities offers them more opportunity
for genuinely being and growing to be themselves than at
any time in history. The pains of discontinuity and distraction are quite real, but they are "growing pains" rather
than the symptoms of a fatal illness.

Admittedly, this multiplicity presents real problems of
organization and self-discipline. If women are to come
closer in our time to a truthful expression of their full
potentialities, they must work for it. It will demand not
artless self-expression, but more precise and disciplined
choices in many areas of their lives. It is becoming more
and more clear which of these choices are critical, and
why. We have attempted to discuss the choices women
must make in such major areas as higher education and
the time of preparation for marriage, adaptations of outside work appropriate for married women, such as part-
time jobs, and the use of leisure.

All of these areas are so closely connected and inter-
dependent that it may be worth stressing again that it is
the first area which is usually decisive. The woman who

marries young, without an adequate period of preparation and education, not only jeopardizes her chances for a viable marriage, but for her own full development as a person. At some future time, many options in leisure and work which must now be sought out with some difficulty may become channeled and institutionalized. "Continuing" higher education might become as subsidized, and as readily available in most localities, as the present high school education. Automation may multiply the opportunities for shorter, part-time working days. But at present, the working out of a complex life pattern is difficult enough to penalize the immature and unprepared. The young woman who has not had the time to form some provisional notion of who she is and what she might become is unlikely, after marriage, to make the disciplined choices in her use of free time that would lead to inner growth rather than diversion; for ordinarily the basis for this self-knowledge must be laid before and not after marriage. The "distracted life" is not conducive to beginning this kind of exploration, and only a "late" marriage by present-day standards will be likely to provide the necessary time: time for education and testing out various vocational possibilities, for direct experience in work for the world, and for specific preparation for the practicalities of domestic life.[3]

Not only does a young woman need time—she urgently needs good sense and discrimination on the part of her

[3] Sidonie Gruenberg and Hilda Krech have suggested that students make boarding arrangements with a family during at least one year in college in return for a certain amount of housework and child care. Obviously, a diversified preparation for marriage should include some expedient of this kind if there has not been adequate training and experience at home.

advisers. At no other time will counseling to help work out her multiple lives be more important. The counseling of women in their forties and fifties is too often only remedial, attempting somewhat vainly to compensate for mistakes made decades earlier. Good sense, moreover, means first of all a recognition of the diversity not just among women as a whole, but within the individual. A young woman, for instance, who has a gift for advanced mathematics and wants very much to marry and raise her own children, cannot be counseled simply as "intellectual" or "future mother." She does not need to be warned of the "trap of domesticity" or exhorted on the "vocation of motherhood." What she needs is practical advice from someone who will accept the simple fact that she likes both children and symbolic logic, and can help her to envision a life that includes both. She needs to know what sort of opportunities in her field might be compatible with part-time work, and what kind of study is likely to be needed in completing her training or keeping it current. On the other hand, she needs to know more of what her children are likely to demand of her at specific stages in *their* lives, so that she can better understand why it is not only her own abilities and interests, however legitimate, that will determine her course. Sensitivity to the needs of one's children does not depend on the presence or absence of outside interests, but it does determine the way in which such interests are pursued.

It has been suggested that young women be guided towards seeing their future life-pattern as a "life in layers," a layer of intellectual life, followed by motherhood and domesticity, with a final layer of productive work in the world. Thus if a woman is really a complex being, with the capacity for multiple lives, she is to be guided to lead these lives in orderly succession. The dangers in such a view, if it is not carefully qualified, should be self-evident. If there is not, for instance, an area of preparation within each "layer" for the next layer or life stage, one is simply faced with the familiar difficulties of the discontinuous life. What is less evident at first sight, but far more important is the need for a wholeness of life *within* each stage, binding together, at least in miniature, those areas of genuine interest that dominate the other stages. Since ministering to the life of her family means more than just keeping its members clean and fed, the continuing intellectual development of the married woman is not selfishness, nor is her involvement in the community a deprivation of her own family. Indeed, this must be put more strongly. The woman who brings a good mind and a generous heart to marriage, and then allows that mind to stagnate and the sphere of her generosity to contract to the size of her family, robs her husband and children as well as herself. This is not the vocation of motherhood, and neither is there some future "layer" of life in which she can be sure of regaining what she has lost.

A "second life," distinct in character or notable in outward achievement, is neither a necessity nor a certainty for every woman. Certainly, for many women a life-stage centered outside the home is either a mirage which comes no closer with middle age, or a possibility which does not interest them, for reasons as various as a new baby, a serious illness, or a major interest, such as care of foster children, which continues to be centered in the home.

This does not mean that a woman for whom a distinct "second life" seems elusive should settle for a narrow horizon and a contracted spirit. In the first place, unlike Mrs. Friedan's discontented heroine, casting a melancholy look at the peanut-butter sandwiches and the Cub Scout car pool as she murmurs "Is this all?," she may feel that helping the human race become human is indeed a very large all. But secondly, God forbid that any woman of good sense regularly submit herself to lunching on peanut butter and ferrying Cub Scouts; breaking out in great bleeding blisters would be the logical outcome. She is just as free as the woman who eventually moves into a major phase of work in the world to use the discretionary time available to her with intelligence, generosity, and purpose. Leisure and education are as important to the woman whose youngest child leaves home when she is sixty as to the more typical mother who reaches that point around forty. It may be even more important to the child of such a mother that she have such a "counterpoise."

The significance of the "second life," therefore, lies not so much in its existence as a separate life-phase as in the presence of the commitments which it represents to a world beyond the home *throughout* married life. Without such commitment, it becomes the dubious gift of some extra years to be filled with some form of harmless occupational therapy. Commitment need not mean competition, the drive to place a definite "mark on the wall" not a millimeter lower than man's. The unmeasurable personal world of married women is still so central, that the more evident mark which they make is not meant for comparison, and can only be distorted in the effort to make it such. For the Christian woman, the "second life" should be woven with the first, expressing more or less visibly an extended concept of her vocation, not its repudiation. Change has not eroded her devotion to her family, but calls her to a more adequate expression of her full possibilities as a human being, and to a widened area for her love.